Mind-Blowing Facts for Curious Kids

The Ultimate Fact Book with 830+ Incredible
Stats and Fun Facts in Science, History, Pop
Culture, and More for Kids Ages 6+

Written and Published by Blaire Ingram

Table of Contents

Introduction

My Purpose for this Book

In an age where information is abundant and readily accessible, statistics serve as the foundation for understanding our complex world. In this book, I aim to bring the most fascinating, insightful, and thought-provoking statistics to light, showing how numbers tell stories, reveal trends, and uncover truths that might otherwise go unnoticed. Whether you're a lifelong learner, a trivia enthusiast, or simply curious about the world, this collection is designed to educate, entertain, and inspire. I'm also aware of the many other books of this type that present uncited, untrustworthy, and unsuitable information and this book aims to be the exact opposite of this. Everything you read in this book has been thoroughly researched and cited to ensure that you all receive only the facts (and that they are perfectly suitable for kids)!

Why Statistics Matter

Statistics go beyond mere numbers; they shape how we view the world and make decisions. Consider how data informs critical policies, drives innovation, and enhances our everyday lives. From forecasting the weather to pushing medical discoveries, statistics is important in bringing order to the complexities of the world. They reveal patterns, highlight connections, and guide better decision-making. In an age where data shapes nearly every aspect of life, understanding and interpreting statistics isn't just valuable—it's essential.

Overview of the Categories

This book is divided into ten engaging categories, each focusing on a unique facet of life, society, and the universe:

- **Science and Technology**
- **Health and Wellness**
- **Education and Learning**
- **Economics and Finance**
- **Pop Culture and Entertainment**
- **Environment and Sustainability**
- **Sports and Athletics**
- **Human Behavior and Psychology**
- **History and Geography**
- **Innovation and Invention**
- **Arts and Creativity**
- **Transportation and Mobility**
- **Ethics and Philosophy**
- **Global Politics and Diplomacy**
- **Family and Relationships**
- **Languages and Linguistics**
- **Fashion and Design**
- **Food and Culinary Arts**
- **Mythology and Legends**
- **Adventure and Exploration**
- **Crafts and DIY Projects**
- **Aviation and Aerospace**
- **Personal Development and Success**

Through these categories picked by yours truly, you'll gain a deeper appreciation for the world's diversity and complexity. Each chapter is packed with intriguing stats and facts that reveal the many intricacies that statistics show in our daily lives.

Key Things to Know Before Reading

While this book is geared toward children and teens, I understand that some terms in the book may be a bit challenging for some individuals. Due to this, I encourage you all to search up terms on your browser of choice!

Also, keep in mind that facts and statistics change over time! This book should contain fairly up-to-date information, but this may change as the years, months, or even days pass! Remember that you should always stay informed from multiple sources and build your own knowledge base!

Now, let's get ready to embark on a journey of discovery, where numbers illuminate the wonders of our world and empower you to think critically, act wisely, and marvel at the fascinating patterns that shape our lives!

Possible Amazon Review?

As a small indie publisher, reviews are hard to come by, as many readers don't leave reviews even if these books have provided them with so much.

I would love it if you could leave a review for the book on Amazon once you are done reading! This will only take around 2-5 minutes of your time, and it would help me a ton and help me keep providing wonderful pieces of content for you all! Much love, and thanks again for supporting me by purchasing this book!

Freebies!

As thanks for purchasing this book, you now have access to a wide array of bonus materials that will provide hours of fun and enjoyment! You'll also have access to an email list where we provide even more goodies, such as coloring pages and activity sheets weekly, at no extra cost! Thanks again for supporting me on this indie publishing adventure!

To access your free bonus materials:

1. Scan the QR code below using your phone's camera (or QR code scanner app).
2. Fill in the short form with your details.
3. Instantly download your bonus resources and sign up to our email list for more coloring pages, activity sheets, and other freebies weekly!

Chapter 1: Science and Technology

Science and technology are like magical tools that help us understand and shape the world around us. From exploring space to making cool gadgets, these wonders make our lives better and more exciting. In this chapter, we'll dive into amazing facts about space, gadgets, the human body, and even the robots that help us do incredible things.

Space Exploration

Space exploration expands our understanding of the universe and drives technological innovation. It inspires curiosity and helps solve challenges on Earth. Here are key statistics that highlight its impact:

- **Earth's neighbors**: Did you know that Venus is the hottest planet in our solar system? It reaches temperatures of about 900°F (475°C), hot enough to melt lead!

- **Biggest star**: The biggest star we know of, UY Scuti, is so massive that over 1,700 Suns could fit inside it. Its radius is about 1,700 times that of our Sun.

Fun Fact #1

Space suits are like mini spaceships! They keep astronauts safe from extreme heat, cold, and even tiny bits of space dust zooming around.

- **Mars facts**: Mars is home to Olympus Mons, the largest volcano in the solar system. At 13.6 miles (22 km) high, it's nearly three times taller than Mount Everest.

- **The Moon landing**: In 1969, Neil Armstrong became the first person to walk on the Moon. Over 400,000 people worked on the Apollo program to make this mission possible.

- **Space stations**: Since 2000, more than 260 people from 20 countries have lived and worked aboard the International Space Station (ISS), orbiting Earth at 17,500 mph (28,000 km/h).

- **Rockets**: Modern rockets, like SpaceX's Falcon 9, can travel faster than 17,000 miles per hour, making space travel possible. That's over 20 times faster than a speeding bullet!

- **Black holes**: Black holes can have masses millions of times greater than the Sun. For example, the black hole at the center of our galaxy, Sagittarius A*, has a mass about 4 million times that of the Sun.

- **Galaxies**: The Milky Way contains over 100 billion stars, and the observable universe has at least 2 trillion galaxies. That's more galaxies than grains of sand on all Earth's beaches!

- **Time travel theories**: Scientists studying Einstein's theories of relativity believe bending space-time might one day make time travel a theoretical possibility.

Incredible Gadgets and Inventions

Incredible gadgets and inventions shape the way we live, work, and play by solving problems and sparking creativity. Here are key statistics that highlight their impact:

- **Smartphones**: A smartphone today has more computing power than NASA's Apollo-era computers, which had only 4 kilobytes of memory.

- **GPS magic**: GPS relies on a network of at least 24 satellites, ensuring accuracy within a few meters anywhere on Earth.

- **Microwaves**: Microwaves work by making water molecules in food vibrate at 2.45 billion times per second, heating it up quickly.

- **Electric cars**: As of 2023, over 26 million electric cars are on the road worldwide, reducing CO_2 emissions by millions of tons annually.

- **3D printing**: 3D printers can create objects layer by layer, including medical prosthetics and even parts of buildings.

- **Drones**: By 2025, the drone industry is expected to be worth over $63 billion, helping with deliveries, farming, and disaster relief.

- **Smartwatches**: Over 200 million smartwatches were sold worldwide in 2022, showing how popular they've become for tracking fitness and health.

- **Augmented reality (AR)**: AR glasses project virtual images into the real world, a technology expected to be a $50 billion market by 2030.

The Human Body: A Living Machine

The human body is an amazing living machine, performing millions of functions every second to keep us alive and thriving. Here are key statistics that highlight its incredible design:

- **Super-fast brain**: The human brain can process information in as little as 13 milliseconds, faster than the blink of an eye.

- **Memory facts**: Your brain can store about 2.5 petabytes of information, equivalent to 2.5 million gigabytes or roughly 3 million hours of TV shows.

- **Neurons**: The brain has around 86 billion neurons, each connecting to thousands of others, forming a network with trillions of connections.

- **Hardworking heart**: Your heart pumps about 2,000 gallons of blood daily, enough to fill a large swimming pool.

- **Blood journey**: Blood travels about 12,000 miles every day, roughly the distance of driving from New York to Los Angeles and back twice.

Fun Fact #2

Your stomach gets new skin every few days because it works so hard to digest food— it's like having a brand-new stomach every week!

- **Blood cells**: In a single drop of blood, there are about 5 million red blood cells, carrying oxygen to every part of your body.

- **Strong skeleton**: Human bones are five times stronger than steel of the same density. They can withstand forces of up to 18,000 pounds per square inch.

- **Muscle power**: Smiling uses 17 muscles, while frowning uses 43, making smiling the easier choice!

- **Growing bones**: Bones stop growing by the age of 25, but they constantly rebuild, replacing themselves every 10 years.

Robots and Artificial Intelligence (AI)

Robots and AI are revolutionizing industries by automating tasks, improving efficiency, and enhancing human capabilities. Here are key statistics that highlight their impact:

- **Robot helpers**: Robots like Roombas clean millions of homes worldwide, while medical robots assist in over 1 million surgeries annually.

- **Rescue robots**: Robots like those used in earthquake zones can locate survivors in rubble faster than human teams.

- **Voice assistants**: As of 2023, over 500 million devices use voice assistants like Alexa, Siri, and Google Assistant.

- **Smart cars**: Self-driving cars, powered by AI, have driven millions of miles in tests, aiming to reduce accidents by up to 90%.

- **Game champs**: AI systems like AlphaGo have beaten world champions in games like Go, chess, and Dota 2.

- **Humanoid robots**: Robots like Honda's ASIMO can walk, climb stairs, and even play soccer, showing the future potential of human-like machines.

- **Nano-robots**: Tiny robots, smaller than a grain of sand, are being developed to deliver medicine directly to diseased cells.

- **Learning robots**: Modern AI systems can learn from their mistakes, improving performance over time, just like humans.

Fun Fact #3

AI can learn to recognize animals just like kids do! For example, if you show an AI pictures of cats and dogs over and over, it learns to tell the difference between them.

Chapter 2: Health and Wellness

Health and wellness are all about how we take care of our bodies and minds. Staying healthy helps us grow stronger, live longer, and enjoy life to the fullest. Did you know that small daily choices, like eating fruits or playing outside, can make a big difference? In this chapter, we'll explore amazing facts about nutrition, exercise, mental health, sleep, and global health trends. Get ready to learn how being healthy can also be fun!

Nutrition and Healthy Eating

Nutrition and healthy eating are essential for fueling the body and mind, supporting growth, and preventing illness. Here are key statistics that highlight their importance:

- **Colorful diets**: Studies show that people who eat at least five different colors of fruits and vegetables each day have a 31% lower risk of chronic diseases, like heart problems and diabetes.

- **Color power**: Each color in fruits and vegetables provides unique nutrients essential for your health. For example, orange carrots are rich in beta-carotene, which the body converts into vitamin A to support vision, skin, and immune function—just one medium carrot provides over 200% of your daily vitamin A needs!

- **Five a day**: Experts recommend eating five servings of fruits and vegetables daily, but most kids only eat three. Adding one extra serving can make a big difference in overall health!

- **Blueberries, the brain boosters**: Research shows that kids who eat blueberries improve their memory and focus by up to 20% during school tests.

- **Milk and bones**: Drinking two glasses of milk daily provides enough calcium to help kids' bones grow stronger. Did you know your bones hold 90% of their calcium by the time you're 12?

- **Nuts and seeds**: A single handful of almonds provides 37% of the vitamin E you need every day, which is great for your skin and immune system.

- **Pizza power**: Did you know that 350 slices of pizza are eaten every second in the U.S.? It's one of the most popular foods in the world.

- **Too much sugar**: On average, kids in the U.S. consume 19 teaspoons of sugar daily—almost three times the recommended amount. Reducing sugar can lower the risk of cavities and diabetes.

- **Healthy swaps**: Replacing one sugary soda with water every day saves 10 pounds of sugar in a year and reduces calorie intake by over 54,000 calories!

Fun Fact #4

Did you know that eating just one apple a day can give you about 4 grams of fiber? That's almost 20% of the fiber you need in one day, helping keep your tummy happy and healthy!

Exercise and Physical Activity

Exercise and physical activity are the keys to a healthy body and mind, boosting energy, mood, and overall well-being. Here are some stats that show just how important staying active is:

- **How much is enough**: Kids should aim for 60 minutes of physical activity each day, but only 1 in 4 actually reach this goal.

- **Fun activities**: Jumping rope can burn about 10 calories a minute, making it one of the best activities for quick bursts of energy.

- **Walking wonders**: Walking 10,000 steps daily equals nearly 5 miles. Most kids only take about 4,500 steps—less than half the goal!

- **Teamwork pays off**: Kids who play team sports are 20% more likely to get better grades in school and have higher self-confidence.

- **Swimming skills**: Swimming uses all the major muscle groups in your body, and an hour of swimming burns around 400 calories.

- **Dancing for fitness**: Dancing can burn as many calories as jogging—about 300 calories an hour. Plus, it's fun!

- **Hula hooping**: Spinning a hula hoop for 10 minutes burns around 100 calories and strengthens core muscles.

- **Video games that move you**: Active video games like Just Dance or Wii Sports help kids burn up to 300 calories per hour while having a blast.

Mental Health and Happiness

Mental health and happiness are the keys to feeling your best and tackling life's challenges with a smile. Here are some stats that show why they matter:

- **Smiling stats**: Smiling releases endorphins that lower stress by up to 30%, and it makes you more approachable, too.

- **Gratitude grows happiness**: Writing down three things you're thankful for every day can increase happiness levels by 25% in just two weeks.

- **Helping others**: Volunteering for just two hours a week can boost happiness and lower stress by up to 20%.

- **Deep breaths**: Slow, deep breathing reduces heart rates and stress levels by 10% in just five minutes.

- **Nature walks**: Spending just 20 minutes in nature can lower cortisol levels, a stress hormone, by 20%.

- **Laughter is medicine**: Laughing for 10 minutes not only lifts your mood but also burns about 40 calories.

- **Making friends**: Kids with strong friendships are 50% more likely to report feeling confident and happy.

- **Family time**: Sharing meals as a family at least four times a week reduces stress and improves communication by 20%.

Fun Fact #5

Playing with pets can boost happiness! Petting a dog or cat for just 5 minutes can reduce stress hormones by 30%!

The Science of Sleep

Sleep is like a superpower—it helps your body recharge and your brain stay sharp. Here are fascinating facts about why snoozing is so important:

- **Growing while snoozing**: Kids need 9–11 hours of sleep each night to grow and stay healthy. Missing sleep slows down your body's ability to repair itself.

- **Sleepy brains**: Losing just one hour of sleep reduces focus and memory by 20%, making it harder to do well in school.

- **Dreaming facts**: On average, people dream for about two hours each night, even if they don't remember it. Dreams help process emotions and thoughts.

- **No screens before bed**: Using a screen within an hour of bedtime reduces melatonin levels by 23%, making it harder to fall asleep.

- **Bedtime routines**: Going to bed at the same time each night can improve sleep quality by 30%.

- **Comfy beds**: Did you know koalas sleep for up to 18 hours a day? While we don't need that much, having a cozy bed can help you sleep better.

Fun Fact #6

When you sleep, your body repairs itself. It helps you heal, grow, and get stronger—just like plugging in a phone to charge!

Global Health Trends

Global health trends are shaping the future of well-being, from fighting diseases to improving access to healthcare. Here's why staying on top of these trends is key to building a healthier world:

- **Clean water saves lives**: Over 90% of the world has access to clean water, but 771 million people still lack it. Clean water reduces disease by 25%.

- **Vaccines work**: Vaccines have decreased diseases like polio and measles by over 80% worldwide.

- **Healthy living**: Japan has the highest life expectancy at 85 years, thanks to their healthy diets rich in fish, rice, and vegetables.

- **Active kids**: In Finland, kids get 15 minutes of outdoor play every hour at school, improving focus by 20%.

- **Healthy schools**: Countries like Sweden provide free school lunches, improving kids' overall health and learning outcomes.

- **Sports worldwide**: Soccer, the world's most popular sport, has over 250 million players across 200 countries.

- **Hunger facts**: Around 9% of the world's population, or about 800 million people, don't have enough food to eat.

- **Pollution problems**: Air pollution affects 90% of people globally, contributing to 7 million deaths annually. Planting trees helps clean the air.

- **Helping hands**: Groups like UNICEF have provided vaccines to nearly half the world's children, saving millions of lives.

Chapter 3: Education and Learning

Education is like a treasure chest that helps you unlock your potential. It's about learning new skills, exploring the world, and getting ready for the future. Did you know that kids spend thousands of hours in school during their lives? This chapter will dive into amazing stats about schools, technology in classrooms, how students learn best, and what's happening in education around the world. Let's get started on this learning adventure!

School Facts and Figures

Schools are where dreams start! From class sizes to cool programs, here are fun facts about what makes schools tick:

- **School days add up**: Kids spend about 6 hours a day in school. Over one year, that's 1,080 hours, or about 45 days of nonstop learning!

- **Attendance matters**: Students who miss 10% or more of school days are 30% less likely to graduate on time.

- **Homework stats**: Kids in the U.S. spend about 6 hours a week on homework, but in Finland, where schools focus less on homework, students still score high on tests.

- **Big or small**: The average public school in the U.S. has about 500 students. Some schools have fewer than 50 students, while others have thousands!

- **Classroom sizes**: On average, there are 24 kids in a classroom in the U.S. Smaller class sizes can help kids learn better.

- **The world's biggest school**: City Montessori School in India has over 55,000 students—imagine how long recess would take!

- **Longest school year**: Japan has one of the longest school years, with about 220 days. The U.S. has around 180 school days.

- **School lunches**: In France, school lunches can last up to two hours, and kids often eat three-course meals!

Learning Styles and Strategies

Everyone learns differently, and that's what makes it exciting! Here are some stats that highlight the best ways to discover your learning superpowers:

- **Visual learners**: Around 65% of kids learn best by seeing pictures, videos, and diagrams.

- **Hands-on activities**: Kids remember up to 75% of what they learn by doing, like building a science project or acting in a play.

Fun Fact #7

Did you know that kids in Japan clean their own classrooms every day? It's part of their lessons to teach responsibility and teamwork!

- **Group learning**: Working with friends can boost learning by 25% because it makes the process more fun and interactive.

- **Reading time**: Kids who read for just 20 minutes a day are exposed to 1.8 million words a year.

- **Journaling power**: Writing in a journal can improve your memory by up to 15% and helps you express your thoughts.

- **Typing vs. handwriting**: Studies show that writing by hand can help you learn better than typing because it involves more brain activity. In fact, research found that students who handwrite notes remember more information and perform 25% better on tests compared to those who type their notes!

- **Repetition works**: Reviewing something three times over a week can improve your chances of remembering it by 60%.

- **Sleep and learning**: Getting a good night's sleep helps your brain store new information. Skipping sleep can lower your test performance by 30%.

- **Study breaks**: Taking a 5-minute break every 25 minutes can help you focus better and learn faster.

Fun Fact #8

Kids who love to move around are called kinesthetic learners. They remember things better when they can act them out or use their hands—perfect for games and experiments!

Technology in Education

From virtual classrooms to fun learning apps, technology is transforming how students learn. Here are some amazing ways it's changing education:

- **Screen time stats**: Over 90% of schools in the U.S. use computers in the classroom. However, spending more than 2 hours on screens outside school can make it harder to focus.

- **E-books vs. textbooks**: E-books are lighter to carry and can save schools up to $250 per student each year.

- **Online learning**: By 2022, about 64% of students worldwide had taken at least one online class.

- **Learning through games**: Educational games can increase learning outcomes by 23%. Minecraft, for example, is used in over 7,000 classrooms.

- **Spelling bee champs**: Apps like Spelling Bee Ninja can help kids improve their spelling skills by 30%.

- **Math made fun**: Math games like Prodigy help kids practice numbers while having fun. Kids using Prodigy solved 50% more math problems than those who didn't.

- **Learning in 3D**: Studies show that using VR can boost information retention by up to 30% because students are immersed in an interactive environment, making lessons feel real and memorable.

- **Field trips from home**: With VR, over 60% of teachers report that virtual field trips improve engagement by allowing kids to explore places like the pyramids of Egypt or the depths of the ocean—all from the comfort of the classroom.

- **Science in action**: VR enables hands-on learning like never before, allowing kids to safely interact with volcanoes, the solar system, and the human body. Research indicates that students using VR for science lessons perform up to 20% better on tests compared to traditional methods.

Global Education Trends

Education trends are connecting the world, from new teaching styles to better access for students everywhere. Here are some highlights shaping the future:

- **Reading worldwide**: About 87% of people in the world can read and write, but in some countries, only 1 in 3 kids goes to school.

- **Girls in school**: Educating girls can increase a country's economy by up to 12%. In some places, girls are still less likely to attend school than boys.

- **Libraries grow learning**: Public libraries in the U.S. lend out 2.2 billion books each year—that's about 7 books for every person!

- **Global enrollment**: About 91% of kids worldwide are in primary school, but only 66% go on to high school.

- **Remote learning**: During the pandemic, over 1.6 billion kids learned from home using computers and the internet.

- **School supplies**: In low-income countries, providing free school supplies can increase attendance by 20%.

- **Hogwarts-inspired**: Some schools in England have houses and competitions, much like in Harry Potter. In fact, over 50% of UK secondary schools reportedly use house systems to encourage teamwork, with competitions ranging from sports to academics.

- **Oldest school**: The University of Karueein in Morocco, founded in 859 AD, holds the Guinness World Record as the oldest continuously operating educational institution. It has educated scholars for over 1,100 years and still thrives as a university today!

- **Green schools**: Eco-friendly schools built from bamboo and recycled materials are on the rise! In Bali, Indonesia, the famous Green School uses 85% locally-sourced bamboo for its construction and incorporates sustainability lessons into its curriculum, inspiring over 500 students from 40 countries.

The Future of Learning

Imagine a world where learning is fun, personalized, and available to everyone. The future of learning is full of possibilities—here are some stats to prove it:

Fun Fact #9

In some countries, kids walk more than 3 miles every day to get to school!

- **AI tutors**: Robots are starting to help kids learn math and languages. Studies show AI tutors can improve learning by up to 40%.

- **Classroom helpers**: In forward-thinking schools, robots assist with tasks like taking attendance, grading papers, and even teaching coding. Research shows that classrooms integrating robotics can increase student engagement by 20-30% in STEM subjects.

- **Cool fact**: Pepper, a robot teacher in Japan, can answer questions and even tell jokes to keep kids interested. This innovative robot can answer questions, tell jokes, and keep kids entertained while they learn. In pilot programs, Pepper has been shown to boost classroom participation rates by up to 25%!

- **Learning your way**: Technology can now adapt lessons to each student's strengths, making studying up to 50% **more effective** and increasing information retention by 25%-60% compared to traditional methods.

- **Smart apps**: Apps like Duolingo adjust lesson difficulty based on your progress. In fact, users who practice consistently with adaptive learning tools are 34% more likely to achieve their learning goals.

- **Digital report cards**: Schools using real-time digital updates improve parent engagement by 85%, helping them stay informed about their child's achievements and areas for improvement.

- **Solar-powered learning**: Schools with solar panels not only reduce carbon emissions but also save money. For example, one solar-powered school in India saves $3,000 annually on electricity, while the U.S. could save over $4 billion per year if all schools adopted solar power.

- **Paperless classrooms**: Switching to digital learning can save up to 30 trees per school each year—that's roughly 75,000 sheets of paper per classroom annually!

- **Outdoor classrooms**: Teaching in natural environments can boost student focus by 20% and improve well-being, with students spending time outdoors showing higher creativity and reduced stress levels.

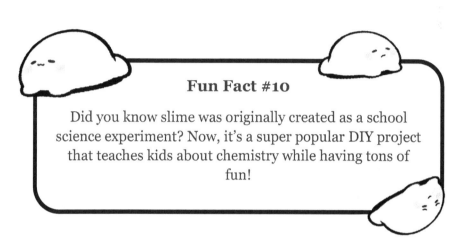

Fun Fact #10

Did you know slime was originally created as a school science experiment? Now, it's a super popular DIY project that teaches kids about chemistry while having tons of fun!

Chapter 4: Economics and Finance

Money makes the world go round, but how much do you really know about it? Economics and finance are all about how people, businesses, and countries use money to buy things, save, and even grow their wealth. This chapter will show you some cool stats about money, saving, spending, and how the world's economy works. Let's dive into the numbers!

The Basics of Money

Understanding money is the first step to mastering the art of managing your life. Here's why knowing the basics is so important:

- **Paper money history**: Did you know the first paper money appeared in China over 1,000 years ago? Today, over 170 currencies are used worldwide.

- **Coins last longer**: Coins can last up to 30 years, while paper bills usually wear out after 6 years.

- **Digital money**: Around 92% of the world's money exists only on computers, not as physical cash.

- **Pocket money**: In the U.S., kids receive an average of $10.50 per week as allowance, often for doing chores.

- **First jobs**: Most people earn their first paycheck at age 16. Babysitting and working at restaurants are common first jobs.

- **Wages around the world**: In Switzerland, workers earn an average of $28 per hour, while in some countries, the average is less than $1 per hour.

- **Biggest bill**: The largest bill ever printed was a $100,000 bill in the U.S., used only for bank transfers.

- **Piggy banks**: The tradition of saving coins in pig-shaped containers started over 600 years ago.

- **Wealthiest person**: Elon Musk's net worth in 2023 was over $200 billion—more than the GDP of some countries!

Saving and Spending

Saving and spending wisely is how we build a secure future and enjoy life today. Check out these stats on how to balance both:

- **Kids saving habits**: About 60% of kids in the U.S. save part of their allowance.

- **Emergency funds**: Experts say you should save enough money to cover 3 to 6 months of expenses, but only 39% of adults have done this.

- **Bank accounts**: Over 80% of adults worldwide have a bank account, but in some countries, fewer than 1 in 3 people do.

Fun Fact #11

Early money wasn't paper or coins. People used things like shells, salt, and even giant stones to trade for goods!

- **Weekly spending**: Families in the U.S. spend an average of $372 per week on food, housing, and transportation.

- **Online shopping**: Online shopping now makes up 20% of all retail sales, up from just 5% a decade ago.

- **Impulse buying**: Studies show that 84% of people have bought something they didn't plan to, which are often candy or snacks at checkout lines.

- **Rule of 50/30/20**: A popular budgeting rule suggests spending 50% of your money on needs, 30% on wants, and saving 20%.

- **School lunches**: Parents spend about $146 per year on average for kids' packed lunches.

- **Biggest expense**: For most families, housing costs take up about 33% of their income.

Economics Around the World

Economics shapes the world we live in, from job markets to trade deals. Here are some key stats that explain why it matters everywhere:

- **Global wealth**: The U.S. is the richest country, with a GDP of $25 trillion in 2023, while Burundi is one of the poorest, with a GDP of $3 billion.

- **Poverty rates**: About 9% of people worldwide live on less than $2.15 a day.

- **Fastest-growing economy**: India's economy grew by 7% in 2022, one of the fastest in the world.

- **Biggest exporters**: China exports $3.5 trillion worth of goods each year, including electronics and clothing.

- **Top imports**: The U.S. spends over $350 billion a year importing oil, cars, and other goods.

- **Food trade**: Brazil is the largest exporter of coffee, providing about 30% of the world's supply.

- **Military budgets**: Countries spent $2.2 trillion on defense in 2022, with the U.S. accounting for 39% of that.

- **Education investment**: The country of Finland spends $11,400 per student each year, which is a ton considering there are some countries spend less than $100.

Fun Fact #12

Did you know there's enough gold in the world to cover the entire planet in a thin layer? That's why gold has been valuable for thousands of years!

- **Health spending**: On average, countries spend 10% of their GDP on healthcare.

Finance and Technology

Technology is changing how we handle money—think digital wallets and crypto! Here's how it's reshaping the world of finance:

- **Bitcoin boom**: In 2023, there were over 420 million cryptocurrency users worldwide, with Bitcoin being the most popular.

- **Fast transactions**: Digital payments like PayPal and Venmo process over 40 million transactions daily.

- **E-wallets**: Over 2 billion people now use mobile wallets instead of cash.

- **Biggest companies**: Apple became the first company worth $3 trillion in 2022.

- **Investing young**: People who start investing at age 20 can have twice as much money by retirement compared to those who start at 30.

- **AI in banking**: About 25% of banks use artificial intelligence to detect fraud.

- **Job changes**: Robots now perform 35% of manufacturing tasks, and this could rise to 50% by 2035.

- **New careers**: Jobs in coding, cybersecurity, and data analysis are growing 12% faster than other fields.

The Future of Money

From digital currencies to new ways to invest, the future of money is exciting. Here are the trends that are changing how we think about cash:

- **Eco-friendly businesses**: Companies that focus on sustainability grew their profits by 29% faster than others in 2022.

- **Green energy jobs**: About 13 million people work in renewable energy, and this number is expected to double by 2030.

- **Recycling trends**: People who recycle regularly save about $120 a year by reducing waste.

- **Mobile banks**: About 76% of people worldwide use mobile apps for banking.

- **Biometric security**: Logging in with fingerprints or facial recognition is becoming increasingly common, with 62% of organizations now using biometric authentication.

- **Learning about money**: Kids who learn how to budget by age 10 are 20% more likely to save money as adults.

- **Allowance lessons**: The parents who take the time to teach their children about how to save see 60% of them grow up to be better with money.

Fun Fact #13

Some countries are already testing digital money called "central bank digital currencies" (CBDCs), which work like video game coins but for real-life spending!

Chapter 5: Pop Culture and Entertainment

Pop culture and entertainment are all around us. From music and movies to video games and viral dances, these fun and exciting parts of life bring people together. Did you know that over 2 billion people around the world play video games? In this chapter, we'll explore amazing facts and statistics about pop culture and entertainment, including how people spend their free time and the incredible ways these industries have grown.

Music and Dance

Music and dance bring joy and connect people in ways words can't. Check out how they're making the world groove:

- **Streaming songs**: Over 500 million people use music streaming services like Spotify and Apple Music every day. In 2023, the most-streamed song had over 3 billion plays!

- **Concert crowds**: Some of the biggest concerts in history had over 1 million people in the audience. That's like 10 football stadiums filled to the brim!

- **K-Pop craze**: BTS, a famous K-pop group, has sold over 30 million albums, making them one of the best-selling bands ever.

- **Dance challenges**: TikTok dance challenges have taken the world by storm. Over 50 million videos have been created for the most popular dance trends.

- **Longest dance marathon**: The record for the longest dance marathon is 126 hours—that's over 5 days of non-stop dancing!

- **Dance in schools**: About 70% of U.S. schools offer dance programs as part of their physical education.

- **Universal tunes**: Studies show that 90% of people around the world listen to music daily, with pop and rock being the most popular genres.

- **Instruments everywhere**: The guitar is the most-played instrument globally, with over 50 million players.

- **Healing music**: Scientists found that listening to music can reduce stress by 68%, making it a powerful tool for relaxation.

Movies and TV Shows

Movies and TV shows entertain, educate, and spark creativity. Here's how they're shaping culture around the globe:

- **Record-breaking movies**: The highest-grossing movie of all time earned over $2.9 billion worldwide. That's more than the GDP of some small countries!

Fun Fact #14

In some countries, people dance to tell stories. For example, hula dancing in Hawaii was originally used to share history and legends!

- **Moviegoers**: On average, about 1.3 billion tickets are sold at movie theaters each year in the U.S. alone.

- **Animation magic**: Animated movies make up 6 of the top 20 highest-grossing films ever.

- **Binge-watching**: Over 60% of people admit to watching an entire TV season in one weekend.

- **Subscribers worldwide**: Netflix, the most popular streaming service, has over 230 million subscribers.

- **Kid-friendly shows**: Shows for kids are some of the most-watched, with over 20 billion hours streamed in 2022.

Fun Fact #15

The first cartoon character with a voice was Mickey Mouse in *Steamboat Willie* (1928). His first words? "Hot dogs!"

- **The Oscars**: Over 40 million people watch the Oscars each year to see their favorite movies and actors win awards.

- **Emmy surprises**: Comedy shows have won the most Emmy Awards, with over 500 wins in the past 20 years.

- **Animated accolades**: Did you know that over 60 animated movies have won Academy Awards since 2001?

Video Games and Digital Fun

Video games and digital fun are the future of entertainment, offering immersive worlds to explore. Here's how they're changing playtime:

- **Global players**: There are over 3 billion gamers worldwide. That's nearly 40% of the planet!

- **Top-selling games**: Minecraft is the best-selling video game ever, with over 240 million copies sold.

- **E-sports excitement**: Competitive gaming events, or e-sports, attract millions of viewers. The 2022 League of Legends World Championship had over 5 million people watching at once.

- **Games on the go**: Mobile games make up 60% of the global gaming market. Popular games like Candy Crush and Roblox have been downloaded billions of times.

- **Time spent playing**: Kids aged 8 to 12 spend about 1.5 hours a day playing mobile games.

- **Educational games**: Over 70% of parents say that mobile games have helped their kids learn new skills.

- **Immersive fun**: Virtual reality (VR) gaming is growing fast, with sales expected to reach $12 billion by 2025.

- **Exploring new worlds**: More than 10 million VR headsets have been sold, allowing players to explore virtual landscapes.

- **Fitness gaming**: VR games like Beat Saber make exercise fun, with players burning up to 600 calories an hour.

Books and Comics

Books and comics open doors to new worlds, ideas, and adventures. Check out why they remain timeless treasures:

- **Bookworms unite**: The average person reads about 12 books a year. That's one book per month!

- **Library lovers**: Over 2 billion books are borrowed from libraries in the U.S. every year.

- **Best-sellers**: The Harry Potter series has sold over 500 million copies worldwide.

- **Superhero stories**: Marvel and DC Comics have sold over 2 billion comics combined.

- **Manga mania**: Japanese manga accounts for about 40% of all comic sales globally.

- **Kids' favorites**: Graphic novels like Dog Man and Diary of a Wimpy Kid are some of the most popular books for kids, selling millions of copies each year.

- **E-books on the rise**: Over 30% of readers prefer e-books, with millions downloaded every month.

- **Audiobooks boom**: In 2022, over 1.5 billion hours of audiobooks were listened to worldwide.

- **Kids and reading**: About 65% of kids aged 6 to 12 read for fun at least once a week.

Celebrities and Social Media

Celebrities and social media bring stars closer to us than ever, changing how we communicate. Here are some stats that show their influence:

- **Biggest stars**: The Rock, Taylor Swift, and Zendaya are some of the most followed celebrities on social media, with millions of fans.

- **Movie magic**: Actors in blockbuster films can earn over $20 million per movie.

- **Record-breaking posts**: The most-liked Instagram post has over 60 million likes!

- **Daily scrolling**: People spend an average of 2.5 hours a day on social media platforms like TikTok and Instagram.

Fun Fact #16

Some celebrities don't run their own social media accounts! They have teams of people who help post content to keep fans updated.

- **Viral videos**: The most-watched YouTube video, Baby Shark, has over 13 billion views.

- **Kid influencers**: Some kids on YouTube earn millions by reviewing toys and games.

- **Fandom facts**: Over 80% of fans say they feel connected to others through their favorite shows, books, or games.

- **Cosplay craze**: Dressing up as characters from movies and games has become a huge hobby, with over 500 cosplay conventions held worldwide each year.

- **Fan fiction fun**: Millions of fan-written stories are shared online, with some becoming so popular they get published as books.

Fun Fact #17

The "Rickroll" prank started as a joke but became a huge internet trend. If you've ever clicked a link and ended up watching *Never Gonna Give You Up*, you've been Rickrolled!

Chapter 6: Environment and Sustainability

The Earth is our home, and it's our job to take care of it. Every small action can make a big difference, from planting trees to recycling. Did you know that every minute, an area of forest the size of 20 football fields is cut down? In this chapter, we'll explore how people and animals share the planet, the importance of renewable energy, and the ways we can help protect nature. Let's learn some amazing stats about the environment and how we can make it better!

Protecting Wildlife

Protecting wildlife keeps ecosystems healthy and our planet thriving. Here's why it's a mission we all should care about:

- **Rainforest homes**: Rainforests are home to over 50% of all the animal and plant species on Earth, even though they only cover about 6% of the planet.

- **Coral reefs**: Coral reefs support 25% of all marine life, but about 50% of reefs worldwide have been damaged due to pollution and climate change.

- **Endangered species**: Every year, over 27,000 species are at risk of extinction. That's like losing 74 species every single day!

- **Elephants**: About 96 elephants are killed every day for their ivory. That's roughly 35,000 elephants each year.

- **Bees**: One out of every three bites of food we eat depends on pollinators like bees, but bee populations have dropped by 40% in the last decade.

- **Tigers**: Fewer than 4,000 tigers are left in the wild today, compared to over 100,000 a century ago.

- **Protected areas**: Over 15% of the world's land and 7% of oceans are protected to help wildlife thrive.

- **Wildlife rescues**: Every year, rescue groups save around 1 million marine animals from fishing nets and trash.

- **Tree planting**: Planting trees creates new homes for animals. Just one tree can provide shelter for up to 300 different species!

Recycling and Waste

Recycling and reducing waste helps protect our planet for future generations. Here's why it's more important than ever:

- **Global waste**: People produce about 2 billion tons of trash each year—enough to fill 800,000 Olympic-sized swimming pools.

- **Plastic problem**: Over 300 million tons of plastic are made every year, but only 9% gets recycled.

- **E-waste**: Electronic waste, like old phones and computers, adds up to 50 million tons a year. That's heavier than all the commercial airplanes ever made!

- **Saving energy**: Recycling just one aluminum can saves enough energy to power a TV for three hours.

- **Water bottles**: Americans throw away about 60 million plastic water bottles every day. Recycling these could save millions of barrels of oil each year.

- **Paper recycling**: Recycling one ton of paper saves 17 trees and enough energy to power a house for six months.

- **Reuse items**: Using a lunchbox instead of disposable bags can save hundreds of bags each year.

- **Pick up trash**: Cleaning up litter can prevent animals from eating or getting stuck in it. Did you know that over 100,000 marine animals and 1 million seabirds die each year from ingesting or becoming entangled in plastic waste? By picking up trash, you help protect wildlife and keep ecosystems healthy!

- **Recycling bins**: Sorting recyclables at home can reduce trash by up to 25%.

- **Garbage in the water**: The world's biggest landfill is the Great Pacific Garbage Patch—an area of floating trash in the ocean that's twice the size of Texas!

Fun Fact #18

Some sneakers, backpacks, and even clothes are made from recycled plastic bottles—so your old water bottle might turn into a cool new jacket!

Climate Change

Climate change is a global challenge, but science and innovation give us hope. Here's why it matters to all of us:

- **Rising temperatures**: The planet has warmed by about 2 degrees Fahrenheit since 1880. That might not sound like much, but it's causing big changes to weather patterns.

- **Melting ice**: The Arctic loses about 13% of its sea ice each decade, which affects polar bears and other animals.

- **Rising seas**: Sea levels have gone up by 8 inches in the past 100 years, and they're rising faster now.

- **Storms**: There are now 50% more hurricanes each year compared to 50 years ago.

- **Wildfires**: On average, wildfires burn about 7 million acres of land each year in the U.S.

- **Solar and wind power**: Renewable energy sources now make up 29% of global electricity. That's up from just 10% two decades ago.

- **Carpooling**: Sharing rides can cut car emissions by 50% or more.

- **Tree planting**: Trees absorb carbon dioxide. Planting 1 trillion trees could remove up to 25% of all the carbon dioxide in the atmosphere.

Renewable Energy

Renewable energy is the key to a sustainable future, helping reduce pollution and protect the planet. Here are the stats that show why it's the way forward:

- **Solar power**: The Sun provides enough energy in one hour to power the entire world for a year. Solar panels are now used by over 2 million homes in the U.S.

- **Wind energy**: Wind turbines produce 10% of the world's electricity, and that number is growing fast.

- **Hydropower**: Dams generate 16% of the world's electricity, enough to power entire countries like Brazil and Norway.

- **Energy savings**: Using energy-efficient light bulbs and appliances can reduce energy use by 50%.

- **Wind power**: The largest wind turbine in the world is taller than the Statue of Liberty and produces enough electricity for 5,000 homes.

Fun Fact #19

The world's largest floating solar farm is in China, and it floats on a lake, proving that solar energy can work even on water!

- **Solar farms**: The world's biggest solar farm in India covers an area larger than 1,400 football fields.

- **Electric cars**: There are now over 26 million electric cars on the road worldwide, saving millions of gallons of gas each year.

Chapter 7: Sports and Athletics

Sports are an exciting way for people to have fun, stay healthy, and even show off their amazing talents. Did you know that over 3.5 billion people around the world watch sports like soccer, basketball, and cricket every year? In this chapter, we'll explore fascinating facts and statistics about popular sports, famous athletes, and even some sports you might not have heard of. Let's dive into the action!

Popular Sports Around the World

From soccer to cricket, sports bring people together worldwide. Here are some fun facts about the sports everyone's talking about:

- **World's favorite sport**: Soccer, or football as it's called in most countries, is played by over 250 million people in more than 200 countries.

- **World Cup fever**: The FIFA World Cup is watched by over 3.5 billion people, nearly half the world's population!

- **Goals galore**: The highest-scoring soccer game ever ended with 149 goals, played in Madagascar in 2002.

- **Global hoop dreams**: Basketball is played by 450 million people worldwide, including kids and pros.

- **The NBA**: The National Basketball Association's 2022 Finals had over 12 million viewers.

- **Tall players**: On average, NBA players are 6 feet 7 inches tall, much taller than the average person.

- **A smashing success**: Cricket is followed by over 2.5 billion fans, mostly in countries like India, Australia, and England.

- **Fastest century**: The record for the fastest 100 runs in cricket is just 31 balls, set by AB de Villiers.

- **Longest matches**: Some cricket matches last up to 5 days, with breaks for tea and meals!

The Science of Sports

The science behind sports helps athletes perform at their best and prevent injuries. Here's how it's changing the game:

- **Getting active**: Kids who play sports are 40% more likely to get the daily exercise they need.

- **Healthy hearts**: Playing sports can lower the risk of heart disease by 30%.

- **Brain power**: Exercise improves memory and learning skills by boosting blood flow to the brain.

- **Fast runners**: Usain Bolt holds the record for the fastest 100-meter sprint at 9.58 seconds. That's faster than most cars in a parking lot!

Fun Fact #20

Basketballs bounce because of air pressure inside them—if you deflate a basketball, it won't bounce as high!

- **High jumpers**: The highest jump ever recorded was 8 feet and 0.5 inches, set by Javier Sotomayor.

- **Longest game**: The longest tennis match lasted 11 hours and 5 minutes, played at Wimbledon in 2010.

- **Sneaky sneakers**: The average pair of running shoes lasts for about 300 miles.

- **Soccer balls**: Over 40 million soccer balls are made every year, enough to circle the Earth twice if lined up.

- **Tennis tech**: Modern tennis rackets increase hitting power by up to 20% compared to wooden rackets.

Famous Athletes and Their Achievements

Famous athletes inspire us with their talent and dedication. Check out how they're breaking records and making history:

- **Gold medalists**: Swimmer Michael Phelps has won 28 Olympic medals, more than anyone in history.

- **Young champs**: The youngest Olympic medalist was just 10 years old, winning in gymnastics in 1896.

- **Global stage**: Over 200 countries compete in the Olympics, with athletes showing incredible talent.

- **Trailblazers**: Serena Williams has won 23 Grand Slam tennis titles, the most in the modern era.

- **Growing leagues**: Women's soccer leagues have grown by 50% in viewership in the last 5 years.

- **Record-breakers**: In 2021, Allyson Felix became the most decorated U.S. track and field athlete with 11 Olympic medals.

- **Young soccer stars**: Many professional soccer players start playing at age 6, and some join pro teams as teens.

- **Skateboarding champs**: At the 2021 Olympics, a 13-year-old won gold in skateboarding.

- **Chess prodigies**: The youngest chess grandmaster earned the title at age 12.

Unusual and Fun Sports

From quidditch to underwater hockey, there are sports that will blow your mind! Here's a look at some of the most fun and unusual:

- **Cheese rolling**: In England, people race down a steep hill chasing a 7-pound (3-kilogram) wheel of Double Gloucester cheese. The cheese can reach speeds up to 70 miles per hour (110 km/h), making the race both thrilling and hazardous. In 2008, 25 participants were injured during the event. If you win, you're able to take home the cheese!

- **Wife carrying**: This funny Finnish sport involves carrying a partner through an obstacle course. The prize? The wife's weight in beer.

- **Four Square**: This playground game is played by millions of kids every day at schools worldwide.

Fun Fact #21

In zorbing, you roll down a hill inside a giant inflatable ball—it's like being inside a human-sized hamster ball!

- **Extreme ironing**: This quirky sport involves taking ironing boards to extreme locations—like mountaintops, underwater, or while skydiving—to press clothes. In March 2008, a team of 72 divers set a world record by simultaneously ironing underwater, which was later broken in 2009 by a team of 86 divers.

- **Dodgeball**: Dodgeball tournaments can include over 1,000 players in a single game.

- **Tag**: Tag has been played for over 2,000 years and is still one of the most popular games for kids.

- **Camel racing**: In the Middle East, camels can run up to 40 miles per hour in races.

- **Pig contests**: At some fairs, pigs compete in obstacle courses. The fastest pig runs 11 miles per hour!

- **Horse jumping**: Showjumping horses can leap over obstacles 7 feet high.

The Future of Sports

The future of sports is all about technology, inclusivity, and global connections. Here's how the games of tomorrow are evolving:

- **Video game champs**: Over 500 million people watch e-sports, and top players can earn millions of dollars.

- **Big tournaments**: The 2021 League of Legends World Championship had 74 million viewers.

- **Pro gamers**: The average age of a pro gamer is just 24 years old.

- **Wearable gadgets**: Smartwatches help athletes track their performance. Over 100 million are sold yearly.

- **Virtual reality training**: VR helps athletes practice skills in a digital world, improving reaction times by 20%.

- **Recycled gear**: Many companies now make sports equipment from recycled plastic, like water bottles. In 2023, Adidas recycled over 50% of its polyester, with a goal to use 100% recycled materials by 2024 in their gear production.

- **Sustainable events**: The 2024 Olympics aim to be carbon neutral, with all energy coming from renewable sources. This effort includes using 100% green electricity and reducing emissions by 50% compared to previous Games, showcasing a new standard for sustainability in global events.

Fun Fact #22

In the future, robots might play sports too! Scientists are already creating robot soccer teams that can dribble, pass, and even score goals.

Chapter 8: Human Behavior and Psychology

Have you ever wondered why people do the things they do or how the brain works? Human behavior and psychology help us understand how we think, feel, and act. Did you know that the average person has about 6,000 thoughts every day? Let's explore fascinating facts and stats about how humans behave and what makes us unique!

How We Think

Our minds are powerful! Understanding how we think helps us unlock our potential and solve problems. Here's why it's important to understand the brain:

- **Brainpower**: The human brain weighs about 3 pounds but uses 20% of the body's energy. It processes information as fast as 120 meters per second, which is faster than most race cars!

- **Gut feelings**: Did you know that 90% of decisions are made using our intuition, or "gut feeling," rather than logic?

- **Dream facts**: About 95% of people dream every night, even if they don't remember it. Dreams can last from a few seconds to 30 minutes.

Fun Fact #23

Your brain processes emotions so fast that you can recognize a happy or sad face in less than a second!

- **Quick choices**: Research shows that people make about 35,000 decisions every day, from what to eat for breakfast to how to solve problems.

- **Memory magic**: On average, people can remember about 7 items in their short-term memory at a time. That's why phone numbers are often 7 digits long.

- **Big decisions**: Choosing a career, buying a home, or making new friends are among the top 10 hardest decisions people face.

- **Attention span**: The average attention span for kids is about 8 seconds—just a little shorter than a goldfish! Practicing focus can make it longer.

- **Multitasking myths**: Studies show that only 2.5% of people can multitask well. Most of us work better focusing on one thing at a time.

- **Screen time**: Kids aged 8-12 spend an average of 4 hours a day on screens, which can affect their focus and sleep.

Emotions and Feelings

Emotions shape how we experience the world and connect with others. Here's why understanding feelings can make life more meaningful:

- **Happiness stats**: Laughing releases chemicals in the brain that make you feel good. Kids laugh about 300 times a day, while adults laugh only 20 times!

- **Feeling blue**: About 1 in 5 kids experience sadness or worry at some point, but talking to friends or family can help.

- **Anger control**: When angry, your heart beats faster, pumping up to 30% more blood than usual. Deep breaths can calm you down.

- **Acts of kindness**: Did you know that doing something kind for someone can make you happier? Studies show that kindness boosts happiness by up to 20%.

- **Volunteering**: About 50% of teenagers volunteer in their communities, helping with food drives, cleanups, and more.

- **Sharing is caring**: Kids as young as 2 years old start to share with others. Sharing helps build strong friendships.

- **Common fears**: About 60% of kids say they're afraid of the dark, spiders, or heights. These fears often go away as they grow up.

- **Facing fears**: When you overcome a fear, your brain rewards you with a feeling of pride and happiness. In fact, studies show that 70-80% of people who confront their fears through exposure therapy experience significant improvement in their anxiety levels.

Fun Fact #24

Your brain never stops working—it's busy even when you sleep, organizing memories and helping you dream!

- **Bravery facts**: Acts of bravery, like standing up for a friend, can inspire others. Surveys show that 80% of kids feel proud after doing something brave.

How We Learn

Learning is the key to growing and achieving our dreams! Here's how understanding the learning process can make us smarter and more creative:

- **Asking questions**: Kids ask an average of 300 questions a day! This curiosity helps them learn and grow.

- **Exploration**: The brain's reward system lights up when we discover something new, releasing dopamine—the "feel-good" chemical. In fact, studies show that dopamine levels can increase by up to 90% during novel experiences, making learning both fun and rewarding!

- **Favorite subjects**: Surveys show that 40% of kids say science is their favorite subject, followed by art and history.

- **Visual learners**: About 65% of people learn best by seeing pictures or diagrams.

- **Hands-on learning**: Around 30% of kids prefer learning by doing activities or experiments.

- **Listening learners**: About 5% of kids find it easiest to learn by hearing stories or explanations.

- **Repetition works**: Studies show that practicing something 20 times makes it stick in your memory.

- **Skill building**: Learning a new skill, like playing an instrument, helps the brain grow stronger connections. Studies show that practicing music can improve memory by 20% and boost problem-solving abilities by up to 30%!

- **Mistakes help**: Making mistakes can improve learning by 30% when we figure out what went wrong.

Relationships and Friendships

Friendships and relationships are the heart of human connection. Here's why they're so important for happiness and well-being:

- **How many friends**: The average person has about 5 close friends, but kids often have many more!

- **Friendship boosts**: Spending time with friends can increase happiness by 50% and reduce stress.

- **Teamwork**: Working with friends on a project or game improves cooperation skills by 70%.

- **Quality time**: Kids who spend at least 30 minutes a day talking to their parents feel 20% happier.

- **Family dinners**: Families who eat together 4 times a week are closer and healthier.

- **Sibling facts**: Having a sibling teaches kids how to share and resolve conflicts. About 80% of kids with siblings say they feel supported by them.

- **Community helpers**: Kids who join clubs or sports teams make new friends 25% faster than those who don't.

- **Acts of generosity**: Giving a small gift or helping someone can create a ripple effect of kindness in a group. In fact, studies show that 60% of people who receive an act of kindness are inspired to pay it forward to someone else, spreading positivity further.

- **Celebrating together**: Sharing birthdays, holidays, or special events with friends and family strengthens bonds. Research shows that families who celebrate together report 35% higher levels of happiness and emotional connection than those who don't.

Fun Fact #25

When you and a friend do something fun together, your heartbeats can sync up without you even noticing!

Chapter 9: History and Geography

History and geography are like a giant storybook and map combined! They tell us all about how the world has changed over time and the amazing places we can explore. Did you know that the Great Wall of China is over 13,000 miles long, or that some cities have been around for thousands of years? Let's dive into the stats and facts that make history and geography so fascinating!

Important Historical Events

History teaches us valuable lessons about the past and shapes our future. Here are some key events that changed the world forever:

- **Moon landing**: In 1969, astronauts Neil Armstrong and Buzz Aldrin became the first humans to walk on the moon. Over 600 million people around the world watched it live on TV!

- **The invention of the printing press**: The printing press was created around 1440. By 1500, about 20 million books had been printed in Europe, spreading knowledge like never before.

- **The fall of the Berlin Wall**: In 1989, more than 2 million people gathered to celebrate the fall of the Berlin Wall, which had divided East and West Berlin for nearly 30 years.

- **The Battle of Hastings**: This battle in 1066 changed England forever. Over 10,000 soldiers fought, and it was one of the most famous battles in European history.

- **The American Revolution**: The 13 American colonies fought for independence from Britain from 1775 to 1783. More than 230,000 soldiers served in the Continental Army.

- **World War II**: Over 70 million people fought in World War II, and it affected nearly every country in the world from 1939 to 1945.

- **The first Olympics**: The ancient Olympic Games began in Greece in 776 BCE and were held every four years. Today, the modern Olympics have athletes from more than 200 countries.

- **Carnival in Brazil**: Every year, millions of people attend Brazil's Carnival, making it the biggest party in the world. It started over 300 years ago!

- **Chinese New Year**: Celebrated by over 1.5 billion people worldwide, this festival marks the start of the lunar calendar.

Fun Fact #26

In the 1800s, some doctors thought ketchup could be used as medicine to treat stomach problems!

Amazing Places on Earth

From the wonders of nature to iconic landmarks, the Earth is full of amazing places. Here's why exploring them matters:

- **Mount Everest**: The tallest mountain in the world is over 29,000 feet high—that's like stacking 20 Empire State Buildings!

- **The Amazon Rainforest**: Covering about 2.1 million square miles, it's home to over 400 billion trees and more species of animals than anywhere else on Earth.

- **The Grand Canyon**: Carved by the Colorado River, this canyon is about 277 miles long and over a mile deep.

- **The Pyramids of Giza**: Built over 4,500 years ago, the Great Pyramid was the tallest structure in the world for nearly 4,000 years.

- **The Eiffel Tower**: This famous Paris landmark is 1,083 feet tall and visited by nearly 7 million people each year.

- **The Great Wall of China**: Stretching over 13,000 miles, it's one of the longest structures ever built. That's about half the length of Earth's equator!

Fun Fact #27

The ancient city of Petra is carved into pink rock cliffs, and its entrance is through a narrow, winding passage that looks like something from a movie!

- **Salar de Uyuni**: Located in Bolivia, this salt flat is the largest in the world, covering over 4,000 square miles. It looks like a giant mirror after it rains.

- **Banff National Park**: Canada's oldest national park has more than 1,000 glaciers and attracts over 4 million visitors a year.

- **Uluru**: This giant red rock in Australia is 1,142 feet tall and holds cultural importance to the local Indigenous people.

Famous Cities and Civilizations

Famous cities and ancient civilizations are the building blocks of our world today. Here's why learning about them is so fascinating:

- **Rome**: Known as the "Eternal City," Rome was founded in 753 BCE. It's home to the Colosseum, which could hold about 50,000 spectators.

- **Machu Picchu**: This ancient Incan city in Peru sits 7,970 feet above sea level and was rediscovered in 1911.

- **Jerusalem**: One of the oldest cities in the world, it has been continuously inhabited for over 5,000 years.

- **Tokyo**: With over 37 million residents, Tokyo is the most populated city in the world.

- **New York City**: Known as the "Big Apple," it's home to over 8 million people and attracts 66 million tourists every year.

- **Dubai**: This city in the UAE has the tallest building in the world, the Burj Khalifa, which stands 2,717 feet tall.

- **The Maya**: This ancient civilization in Central America built amazing pyramids and developed a calendar. At its height, it had a population of over 19 million.

- **The Indus Valley**: One of the world's first urban civilizations, it had cities with over 40,000 people more than 4,000 years ago.

- **Atlantis**: While it might just be a myth, stories of this lost city have fascinated people for centuries. In fact, over 2,400 years ago, the philosopher Plato first wrote about Atlantis in his works Timaeus and Critias.

How Geography Shapes Life

Geography influences where we live, what we eat, and how we interact with the world. Here's why understanding geography is essential:

- **Rainiest place**: Mawsynram, India, gets about 467 inches of rain every year. That's like 39 feet of water!

- **Hottest place**: Death Valley, California, holds the record for the hottest temperature ever recorded: 134°F (56.7°C) in 1913.

- **Coldest place**: Antarctica's temperatures can drop to -128.6°F (-89.2°C), making it the chilliest spot on Earth.

- **Oil production**: Saudi Arabia produces about 10 million barrels of oil each day, making it one of the top oil producers.

- **Water usage**: Humans use about 4 trillion cubic meters of water annually, with agriculture consuming 70% of it.

- **Forests**: Forests cover about 31% of Earth's land area and are home to over 80% of terrestrial species.

- **Urban areas**: Over 56% of the world's population lives in cities, a number expected to rise to 68% by 2050.

- **Languages**: There are about 7,000 languages spoken around the world, but 40% of them are endangered.

- **Transportation**: About 1 billion bicycles are used globally— that's more than double the number of cars!

Fun Fact #28

The first cars didn't have steering wheels— drivers had to steer them using a lever instead!

Chapter 10: Innovation and Invention

Every invention started as a creative idea. From the first wheel to modern smartphones, inventions have changed the way people live, work, and play. Did you know that over 1 million patents are granted worldwide every year? In this chapter, we'll dive into amazing facts and stats about inventions and the people who create them. Get ready to explore the world of innovation!

Famous Inventions That Changed the World

Inventions have transformed the way we live, work, and play. Here's a look at the game-changers that shaped history:

- **Old but gold**: The wheel was invented around 3,500 BCE. That's over 5,500 years ago! Today, wheels are found in cars, bikes, airplanes, and even robots.

- **Spinning numbers**: In the U.S., there are over 275 million vehicles with wheels on the road.

- **Global movement**: Bikes are the most common form of transportation, with over 1 billion bikes worldwide!

- **Shocking discovery**: Thomas Edison invented the first practical light bulb in 1879. Today, there are over 20 billion light bulbs lighting up the world.

- **Powering up**: In 2023, 84% of the world's population had access to electricity, helping billions of people stay connected.

- **Electric inventions**: From refrigerators to smartphones, electricity powers over 50% of the devices people use every day.

- **A connected world**: The internet became popular in the 1990s. Now, over 5 billion people use it daily—that's more than half the world!

- **Fun fact**: Over 300 billion emails are sent every day—enough to circle the Earth 10 times if printed on paper.

- **Streaming boom**: Every minute, people watch over 1 million hours of video on platforms like YouTube and Netflix.

How Inventions Are Created

Inventions start with big ideas and a lot of creativity! Here's how the coolest ideas turn into reality:

- **Dream big**: About 60% of inventors say they got their ideas by observing everyday problems and thinking of solutions.

- **Kids' creativity**: Did you know that kids invent about 5,000 new things each year, like better backpacks and cool games?

- **Trial and error**: On average, inventors test their ideas 50 times before they succeed.

Fun Fact #29

The invention of the lightbulb was a big "bright" idea! Before lightbulbs, people used candles and oil lamps to see in the dark.

- **Famous example**: This moment of inspiration led to the creation of Velcro, which is now a multi-billion-dollar industry. Velcro is used in over 60% of clothing and footwear worldwide!

- **Light bulb lesson**: Thomas Edison tried over 1,000 materials before finding the perfect one for his light bulb.

- **3D printing**: Today, 3D printers help inventors create prototypes 10 times faster than traditional methods.

- **Better together**: Over 70% of successful inventions are created by teams working together.

- **Around the world**: Scientists from over 100 countries worked together to create COVID-19 vaccines.

- **Sharing ideas**: In 2022, over 4 million patents were shared in global databases to help inventors collaborate.

The Coolest Inventions in Recent Years

Innovation is all around us! From smart gadgets to groundbreaking technologies, here's what's rocking the world of inventions:

- **Pocket power**: The first smartphone was created in 1992. Today, there are over 6.8 billion smartphone users worldwide.

- **Amazing apps**: There are over 3.5 million apps available, helping people do everything from learning languages to playing games.

- **Every second counts**: People unlock their phones an average of 150 times a day!

- **Flying high**: Over 2.5 million drones are used worldwide, helping with deliveries, photography, and even rescue missions.

- **Quick deliveries**: In 2022, drones delivered over 2 million packages to people's homes.

- **Saving lives**: Rescue drones helped save over 500 people trapped in dangerous places last year.

> **Fun Fact #30**
>
> The Slinky was invented by accident! A scientist dropped a spring, and when it "walked" down the stairs, he realized it could be a fun toy.

- **Going green**: Over 10 million electric cars were sold in 2022, helping reduce pollution and save energy.

- **Tesla takeover**: Tesla is one of the biggest electric car companies, producing over 1 million cars in 2022 alone.

- **Fast chargers**: Charging stations have grown by 50% in the last five years to keep up with demand.

The Future of Innovation

The future is full of possibilities! Here's a peek at the innovations that will change the world in exciting ways:

- **Mars missions**: NASA and other space agencies plan to send humans to Mars by 2040.

- **Moon base**: Scientists are working on building a moon base that could house 100 people by 2050.

- **Rockets everywhere**: In 2022, there were over 180 rocket launches worldwide, carrying satellites and other tools for space research.

- **Smart helpers**: AI is used in over 50% of businesses to solve problems faster and smarter.

- **Robot teachers**: Some schools now use robots to teach languages and math.

- **Future impact**: Experts predict AI could create over 58 million new jobs by 2030.

- **Green tech**: Solar panels and wind turbines provide over 10% of the world's energy and are growing fast.

- **Ocean cleanup**: In 2023, robots removed over 5 million pounds of trash from oceans.

- **Recycling boost**: Over 1 billion plastic bottles were recycled into new products like clothes and furniture last year.

Fun Fact #31

Some scientists are training seaweed and oysters to help clean the ocean because they naturally absorb pollution!

Chapter 11: Arts and Creativity

Arts and creativity bring color, fun, and excitement to our lives. From drawing and painting to music and movies, people of all ages love expressing themselves in unique ways. Did you know that creative activities help kids and adults learn faster and feel happier? In this chapter, we'll explore amazing facts and numbers about art, music, and creativity from all over the world.

The World of Visual Arts

Visual arts let us see the world in new and colorful ways, sparking imagination and creativity. Here's why they're so impactful:

- **Masterpieces that last**: Did you know that Leonardo da Vinci's *Mona Lisa* is seen by over 10 million people every year at the Louvre Museum in Paris? That's like everyone in New York City taking a trip to see her smile!

- **Popular colors**: Surveys show that blue is the most popular color in paintings, chosen by 40% of artists.

- **Art classes for kids**: Around 70% of schools in the U.S. have art programs, helping kids discover their inner Picassos.

- **Drawing skills**: By age 6, most kids can draw over 10 different shapes, from circles to stars.

- **Craft time**: About 50% of children aged 6-12 in the U.S. love making crafts like friendship bracelets and paper airplanes.

- **Art museums**: Visiting museums is more popular than you'd think—around 850 million people visit art museums worldwide every year!

- **City art**: The longest mural in the world is in Rio de Janeiro, Brazil, stretching over 15,000 square feet—the size of 10 basketball courts!

- **Graffiti styles**: About 20% of street art around the world is made by artists under 18 years old.

- **Brightening neighborhoods**: Studies show that murals can make a city feel 30% more welcoming to visitors.

The Power of Music

Music isn't just sound—it's emotion, memory, and connection wrapped in rhythm and melody. Check out how it changes our lives:

- **Brain boost**: Kids who play an instrument are 40% more likely to do well in math and reading.

- **School bands**: In the U.S., about 12% of kids in middle school play in the school band or orchestra.

- **Worldwide tunes**: Did you know that the *Happy Birthday* song is sung more than 2 billion times each year? That's a lot of birthday cakes!

- **Top picks**: The most popular instruments for kids are the piano (played by 21%) and the guitar (played by 16%).

Fun Fact #32

Some paintings are so big they could cover an entire basketball court!

- **Drum fun**: Playing the drums burns about 200 calories per hour—just like jogging!

- **Music classes**: In Japan, about 95% of elementary schools include music lessons as part of their curriculum.

- **Big crowds**: The largest concert ever had over 3.5 million people in Brazil. That's more than the population of Chicago!

- **Music fans**: Around 30 million kids attend music festivals with their families every year in the U.S.

- **Costumes and lights**: Did you know that some concerts use over 500,000 watts of power just to light up the stage? That's enough to power 100 homes!

Writing and Storytelling

Writing and storytelling let us share adventures, emotions, and ideas that inspire the world. Here's why they're so magical:

- **Books for kids**: The *Harry Potter* series has sold over 600 million copies—enough for every kid in the world to have one!

- **Bedtime stories**: Studies show that kids who read before bed sleep 25% better than those who don't.

- **Libraries rule**: There are about 117,000 libraries around the world, and they lend out millions of books every year.

- **Daily writing**: Around 30% of kids in the U.S. write in a journal every day to keep track of their thoughts and ideas.

- **Kids as authors**: Did you know that kids as young as 8 have written best-selling books? One of the youngest authors, Dorothy Straight, wrote her book at age 4!

- **World's longest story**: The longest novel ever written has over 9.6 million words—that's like reading 10,000 books!

- **Rhymes and rhythms**: About 15% of kids in the U.S. write their own poems in school.

- **World records**: The largest poetry reading involved over 13,000 people reading at the same time.

- **Limericks are loved**: Short and funny poems called limericks are written in classrooms by millions of kids every year.

Dance and Movement

Dance is how the body tells a story, expressing emotions and culture without words. Here's why it moves us:

- **Popular styles**: Did you know that hip-hop is the favorite dance style for 1 in 5 kids in the U.S.?

- **Dancing for health**: Kids who dance for an hour a day are 30% more likely to have strong muscles and bones.

Fun Fact #33

The world's smallest book is so tiny that you need a microscope to read it!

- **Global grooves**: Over 200 countries celebrate traditional dances, like salsa in Cuba or ballet in Russia.

- **Big events**: The largest dance competition had over 8,000 dancers performing at the same time.

- **Trophies and prizes**: About 50,000 dance competitions happen every year in the U.S., from small towns to big cities.

- **Kids in the spotlight**: Over 20% of competitive dancers in the U.S. are under the age of 12.

- **Making moves**: Choreographers can create up to 100 new dance routines in a single year.

- **Improvisation fun**: Kids love freestyle dancing, with 60% saying it's their favorite way to move to music.

- **Music and dance**: Studies show that music helps dancers learn new moves 25% faster.

Fun Facts About Creativity

Creativity makes life more fun, exciting, and full of possibilities. Here are some fascinating facts about the magic of imagination:

- **Brain boosts**: People who do creative activities are 35% more likely to feel happy every day.

- **World's largest painting**: The biggest painting ever made was over 62,000 square feet, created by kids from more than 50 countries!

- **Art for animals**: Did you know that elephants can paint? Some zoos have sold elephant art for over $1,000 to help care for the animals.

- **Color sparks ideas**: The color blue is proven to enhance creative thinking by 20%, while red is better for detail-oriented tasks.

- **The Power of doodling**: People who doodle while listening retain 29% more information, showing that creativity helps focus.

- **Walking fuels ideas**: Taking a walk can increase creative output by up to 60% compared to sitting. Time to hit the trail and brainstorm!

Fun Fact #34

Drawing, dancing, and storytelling aren't just fun—they help your brain grow and become even better at problem-solving!

Chapter 12: Transportation and Mobility

Have you ever thought about how people and things move from one place to another? Transportation is all around us—cars, planes, trains, and even scooters help us get where we need to go. This chapter is full of amazing numbers and facts about how people travel and how vehicles work. Let's take a ride through the world of transportation!

Land Transportation

From bicycles to bullet trains, land transportation keeps us moving and connected. Here's how it's shaping our world:

- **Many, many cars**: There are more than 1.5 billion cars on Earth. If you parked them bumper to bumper, they could circle the planet 50 times!

- **Long road trips**: The average American drives about 13,500 miles every year. That's like going across the U.S. from coast to coast 4 times!

- **Electric cars**: Did you know that over 14 million electric cars are on the road today? That's enough to cut down millions of tons of pollution every year!

- **Bike fans**: Over 1 billion bicycles are used around the world, and about 60% of kids in the U.S. ride bikes regularly.

- **Fast pedals**: The fastest bicycle ride ever recorded was 183.9 miles per hour—faster than most race cars!

- **Scooters zooming**: In cities, electric scooters are super popular, with over 150 million rides happening every year.

- **Subway systems**: Did you know that the Tokyo subway carries more than 8 million people every day? That's more people than the entire population of New York City!

- **Buses to school**: About 25 million kids in the U.S. ride the school bus every day. If all those buses lined up, they would stretch over 10,000 miles!

- **Light rail**: Trains like subways and trolleys reduce car traffic by 25% in busy cities.

Air Transportation

Flying isn't just for birds! Air transportation connects the globe faster than ever. Check out why it's so important:

- **Busy skies**: Around 100,000 flights take off every day worldwide. That's about one flight every second!

- **Longest flight**: The world's longest airplane ride takes about 19 hours, flying from New York City to Singapore— almost halfway around the globe!

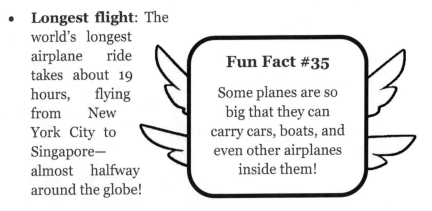

Fun Fact #35

Some planes are so big that they can carry cars, boats, and even other airplanes inside them!

- **Reaching new heights:** Planes fly at around 35,000 feet, which is higher than the tallest mountains on Earth.

- **Whirlybirds**: Helicopters can hover, which is something airplanes can't do. They're used to save lives in about 400,000 rescue missions every year.

- **Fast flights**: The fastest helicopter in the world can fly at 295 miles per hour—as fast as a cheetah running 10 times in a row!

- **Floating high**: The first-ever human flight happened in a hot air balloon in 1783. Today, over 2,000 balloon festivals are held every year around the world!

- **Big balloons**: Some hot air balloons are taller than a 10-story building and can carry up to 16 people.

Water Transportation

Boats and ships have been traveling Earth's waterways for centuries. Here's why water transportation still makes waves:

- **Cargo ships**: Did you know that cargo ships carry about 90% of the world's goods? That includes toys, clothes, and even bananas!

Fun Fact #36

Hovercrafts can glide over both water and land, floating on a cushion of air like a giant air hockey puck!

- **Cruise fun**: Each year, about 30 million people take cruises on giant ships that are like floating cities. Some even have water slides and ice-skating rinks!

- **Fast boats**: The fastest boat ever went over 317 miles per hour—faster than most airplanes during takeoff!

- **Deep dives**: Submarines can go as deep as 36,000 feet into the ocean. That's like stacking 24 Empire State Buildings on top of each other!

- **Military use**: There are about 450 submarines in use by different countries around the world.

- **Science subs**: Scientists use submarines to explore the ocean, and they've discovered over 10,000 new species of sea creatures this way.

- **Wind power**: Sailboats use the wind to move, and people have been sailing for over 6,000 years.

- **Races on water**: The America's Cup, one of the most famous sailing races, started in 1851 and is still held today.

Space Transportation

From rockets to Mars missions, space transportation is taking us where no one has gone before. Here's what makes it out of this world:

- **Blasting off**: Rockets travel at speeds of about 25,000 miles per hour to escape Earth's gravity. That's fast enough to get from New York to London in just 12 minutes!

- **Satellite stats**: There are more than 6,500 satellites orbiting Earth right now, helping with things like GPS and weather forecasts.

- **Astronaut homes**: The International Space Station (ISS) is as big as a football field and orbits Earth about 16 times a day.

- **Floating experiments**: Over 3,000 experiments have been conducted on the ISS, from growing plants to studying how humans adapt to space.

- **Red planet explorers**: NASA's rover *Perseverance* landed on Mars in 2021 and has traveled over 11 miles on the planet's surface, sending back cool pictures and samples.

Future of Transportation

The future of getting around is electric, automated, and eco-friendly. Here's why it's so exciting:

- **Robots on wheels**: About 30 million self-driving cars are expected to be on the road by 2030.

- **Safety first**: Studies show that self-driving cars could reduce car accidents by 90%.

- **Test drives**: These cars are being tested in over 40 cities around the world right now.

- **Super-fast trains**: Hyperloop systems could travel at speeds of up to 760 miles per hour—that's faster than a jet plane!

- **Up in the air**: Companies are working on flying cars, and about 200 prototypes have already been built.

- **Traffic-free travel**: Flying cars could reduce city traffic by 30% in the future.

World Records in Transportation

Fastest, biggest, and most creative—transportation world records push the limits. Here are some incredible achievements:

- **Longest traffic jam**: The world's longest traffic jam happened in China in 2010 and stretched 62 miles long, lasting for 12 days! That's like being stuck in traffic from New York City all the way to Washington, D.C.!

- **Longest train**: The world's longest train is over 4.5 miles long and has more than 600 cars! It's so long that it could fit more than 300 school buses in a single line!

- **Fastest car**: The Bugatti Chiron Super Sport 300+ is the fastest car ever, reaching an incredible speed of 304 miles per hour! That's faster than an airplane on a runway!

- **Longest boat**: The world's longest boat is the Mighty Mo, a super-sized ferry in Japan, measuring 118 meters (387 feet) long—almost the length of two basketball courts!

Fun Fact #37

The tallest bridge in the world is so high up that clouds sometimes pass underneath it!

82

Chapter 13: Ethics and Philosophy

What's right? What's wrong? Ethics and philosophy are all about big questions like these! They help us understand how people think, make choices, and decide how to treat others. Let's dive into some cool stats and stories that show how people think about fairness, kindness, and big ideas!

Ethics in Everyday Life

Doing the right thing can be tricky, but ethics help us navigate our daily choices. Here's why they matter:

- **Telling the truth**: Studies show that 98% of kids believe it's important to be honest, but about 70% of kids admit they've told a lie to avoid getting in trouble at least once.

- **Sharing is caring**: In one experiment, kids aged 6-10 shared 60% of their candy with others when asked, even when they didn't have to.

- **Cheating stats**: About 35% of students say they've cheated on a school assignment. That's why talking about fairness is so important!

- **Random acts of kindness**: A study found that doing kind things, like helping a friend or giving compliments, makes people feel 25% happier.

- **Helping heroes**: In emergencies, more than 75% of people say they would help someone in danger, even if they didn't know them.

- **Volunteer power**: Did you know that 50% of teens in the U.S. volunteer their time to help others every year? That's millions of kids making the world a better place!

- **The Golden Rule**: The Golden Rule says, "Treat others the way you want to be treated." This idea is super old and appears in 21 different major religions around the world!

- **Bullying stats**: Schools with kindness programs based on the Golden Rule see bullying drop by 30%.

- **Friendship boost**: Kids who follow the Golden Rule are twice as likely to have strong friendships.

Philosophical Questions

Big questions make us think deeply about life, the universe, and everything. Here's why philosophy is so fascinating:

- **Happiness around the world**: The United Nations measures happiness every year, and Finland has been ranked the happiest country for 6 years in a row!

Fun Fact #38

"The Ship of Theseus" is a famous thought experiment that asks: If you replace every part of a ship, is it still the same ship? It's quite the puzzling question!

- **Kid joy**: A study showed that 75% of kids say spending time with their family makes them the happiest.

- **Little things matter**: People who practice gratitude, like saying "thank you," are 20% more likely to feel happy every day.

- **Rules or feelings**: About 60% of people say they decide what's right based on rules, while 40% trust their feelings or instincts.

- **Culture and ethics**: In one study, 85% of kids said stealing is always wrong, but when asked if it's okay to steal food if you're starving, only 20% thought it was still wrong.

- **Different types of smarts**: A psychologist named Howard Gardner found there are 8 types of intelligence, like being good at math, art, or understanding others.

- **Curiosity counts**: Studies show that kids who ask more "why" questions are 50% more likely to solve problems creatively.

Ethics in Big Decisions

From laws to life-changing choices, ethics guide us in shaping a better world. Here's how they make a difference:

- **Wildlife care**: About 200 species of animals go extinct every day, but conservation efforts have saved animals like the giant panda.

- **Pet lovers**: 68% of families in the U.S. own a pet, and studies show kids with pets are 30% more likely to feel empathy.

- **Recycling champs**: Kids who recycle at school encourage their families to recycle, too, and schools with recycling programs see a 40% increase in community participation.

- **Screen time choices**: Kids aged 8-12 spend an average of 4-6 hours a day using screens, but families that set rules see 50% less screen time.

- **Kindness online**: About 70% of kids say they've seen mean behavior on the internet, but reporting bad behavior to adults reduces online bullying by 57%.

History of Philosophy

For thousands of years, philosophers have explored life's biggest mysteries. Here's why their ideas still inspire us:

- **Over 2,500 years old**: Philosophy began more than 2,500 years ago, when ancient thinkers like Socrates, Plato, and Aristotle in Greece started asking big questions about life, truth, and happiness.

- **Schools of thought**: There are more than 100 different schools of philosophy around the world, each with unique ideas about how we should live, think, and understand the world.

- **Philosophers everywhere**: Philosophers have come from every continent, with famous thinkers from places like India (like Buddha), China (like Confucius), and Africa (like St. Augustine).

- **Philosophy in schools**: Today, philosophy is taught in over 40 countries as part of school curriculums, helping kids think about life's big questions.

Thinking About the Future

Philosophy helps us imagine and shape a future filled with possibility. Here's why it's more important than ever:

- **Big thinkers**: A survey found that 80% of kids believe they can make the world a better place by helping others and protecting the planet.

- **Creative solutions**: More than 65% of adults say they're hopeful for the future because kids today care so much about fairness, kindness, and big ideas.

- **Start small**: Helping one person makes a big difference. In fact, studies show that doing something kind spreads to 3 other people as they pass it on!

- **Dream big**: People who write down their goals are 42% more likely to achieve them, so start thinking about how you can help others and follow your dreams.

Fun Fact #39

The future will bring new challenges, like AI rights and climate ethics, giving philosophers plenty of exciting new problems to solve!

Chapter 14: Global Politics and Diplomacy

Imagine a world where countries work together to solve big problems, like protecting the environment, ending hunger, or making sure everyone is safe. That's what global politics and diplomacy are all about! Leaders meet, talk, and make decisions to help people live better lives. Let's explore some amazing stats about how countries work together to make the world a better place.

How Countries Work Together

From peace treaties to global goals, countries teaming up makes the world a better place. Here's why cooperation is key:

- **The United Nations (UN)**: It's a group of 193 countries that meet to solve global problems like war, poverty, and climate change. That's almost every country in the world!

- **Helping people in need**: The UN provides food, shelter, and medical care to over 100 million people every year.

- **Peacekeepers**: More than 80,000 peacekeepers from 120 countries help keep people safe in areas where there's conflict.

- **Protecting the planet**: The Paris Agreement is a deal between 195 countries to reduce pollution and stop global warming. Countries in the agreement aim to cut greenhouse gas emissions by 50% by 2030.

- **Saving the oceans**: Over 170 countries have agreed to stop dumping trash into the ocean. This has helped reduce pollution in some areas by as much as 40%!

Elections Around the World

Elections give people a voice in how they're governed. Here's why they're so vital to democracy:

- **Global voters**: Did you know that about 5 billion people around the world are old enough to vote? That's more than half the planet's population!

- **Youth power**: In some countries, like Brazil and Austria, kids as young as 16 can vote in elections.

- **Biggest democracy**: India has the largest number of voters, with over 900 million people eligible to vote in elections.

Fun Fact #40

In India, where many languages are spoken, political parties are represented by symbols like flowers, animals, or everyday objects to help voters identify them easily.

- **Observers on duty**: Organizations like the UN send election observers to over 60 countries to make sure elections are fair and honest.

- **High turnout**: In countries like Australia, they have higher voter turnout rates as compared to the United States. For example, in the 2019 Australian federal elections, about 91.9% of eligible voters cast their ballots.

World Leaders and Diplomacy

World leaders use diplomacy to solve big problems and keep peace. Here's how they make an impact:

- **The Geneva Conventions**: These rules protect soldiers and civilians during war. Over 190 countries have agreed to follow them.

- **Trading goods**: Countries trade items like food, clothes, and electronics. Global trade adds up to about $32 trillion every year!

- **Meet and greet**: World leaders meet at summits like the G7 and G20 to talk about important topics like ending poverty or preparing for natural disasters. For example, the G20 nations represent 85% of global GDP, 75% of international trade, and two-thirds of the world's population, making their decisions critical for global progress.

- **Conflict resolution**: Diplomats help prevent wars by talking and negotiating. Peace talks have reduced global conflicts by 20% in the past decade.

- **The Good Friday Agreement**: This deal ended a long conflict in Northern Ireland and brought peace to the region in 1998.

Fun Fact #41

Some world leaders get fun nicknames! Former British Prime Minister Winston Churchill was called the "British Bulldog" because of his tough attitude during World War II.

Helping People Around the World

From disaster relief to global health efforts, helping others connects us all. Here's why it's so important:

- **Global generosity**: Countries like the U.S., Germany, and Japan give billions of dollars each year to help people in poorer nations. In 2022, about $180 billion was donated worldwide!

- **Disaster relief**: After big disasters like earthquakes or hurricanes, international organizations like the Red Cross help over 25 million people each year.

- **Stopping polio**: A global campaign has helped reduce polio cases by 99%, saving millions of lives.

- **COVID-19 vaccines**: Over 13 billion vaccine doses were given worldwide to help fight the pandemic.

Global Challenges

Climate change, poverty, and pandemics remind us that teamwork is essential. Here's why tackling these challenges matters:

- **Rising temperatures**: The Earth's temperature has gone up by 2°F (1.1°C) since the 1800s, and leaders are working to stop it from rising more than 2.7°F (1.5°C).

- **Clean energy**: Over 170 countries are switching to renewable energy sources like wind and solar power to reduce pollution.

- **Feeding the hungry**: About 9% of the world's population (around 700 million people) don't have enough food to eat. Organizations like the World Food Programme deliver food to about 150 million people every year.

- **School for all**: Globally, about 260 million kids don't go to school. Programs like UNICEF are working to make sure every child has access to education.

Youth and Global Politics

Young voices are shaping the future of politics and global change. Here's why their ideas are worth listening to:

- **Youth voter power**: In the 2020 U.S. presidential election, about 50% of eligible voters aged 18-29 cast their votes, showing how young people are shaping political decisions.

- **Young leaders**: At the age of just 25, Malala Yousafzai became the youngest-ever recipient of the Nobel Peace Prize for her work in advocating for girls' education worldwide.

- **Climate change activism**: Over 1.4 million young people worldwide participated in the Fridays for Future movement, led by Greta Thunberg, to demand action on climate change.

Fun Fact #42

Some towns let kids serve as "Kid Mayors" for a year to learn about government and help with city projects!

Chapter 15: Family and Relationships

Families and friends are some of the most important parts of our lives! They give us love, laughter, and support. But did you know there are all kinds of cool stats about families and relationships? From the way families spend time together to how friendships grow, let's take a look at the numbers behind our closest connections.

Families Around the World

Families look different everywhere but love and support are universal. Here's why they're so special:

- **Big or small**: Families come in all sizes! In the U.S., the average family has about 3 people, but in countries like Senegal, families often have 7 or more people living together.

- **Grandparents rule!** In some countries like India and Mexico, it's common for 3 or even 4 generations to live in the same house. That's like having your grandparents, parents, and cousins all together!

- **Furry friends**: In the U.S., about 70% of families have a pet, with dogs being the most popular (around 50 million households) and cats close behind.

- **Pet-loving countries**: Argentina has the most pet owners, with 80% of families having a furry, scaly, or feathery friend!

Spending Time Together

From game nights to vacations, time spent together builds lifelong memories. Here's why it matters:

- **Dinner time**: Families that eat together are closer! About 88% of parents say eating dinner together helps them bond with their kids.

- **Movie nights**: The average family watches about 20 hours of TV or movies together every week. That's a lot of popcorn!

- **Vacation adventures**: Families in Europe travel the most, with about 75% going on vacation at least once a year.

> **Fun Fact #43**
>
> Listening to stories from parents or grandparents helps kids learn about their family history and strengthens relationships.

- **Chit-chat time**: On average, parents spend 2 hours a day talking to their kids. In Japan, parents focus a lot on school, spending about 60 minutes each evening helping with homework.

- **Bedtime stories**: Reading together is a favorite activity for many families. In the U.S., about 55% of parents read to their kids every night.

Friendships

Friends make life brighter, helping us grow and laugh along the way. Here's why they're so important:

- **Lots of friends**: The average person has about 3-5 close friends they trust and hang out with regularly.

- **First friendships**: Did you know that kids as young as 3 years old start forming their first friendships?

- **Besties forever**: About 40% of people say they've been best friends with someone since childhood.

- **Playing together**: About 70% of kids say they love playing outside with their friends, like riding bikes or playing tag.

- **Video games**: Almost 60% of kids around the world play video games with friends, either in person or online.

- **Sharing secrets**: Over 80% of kids say they trust their best friend the most when they have something important to share.

Fun Fact #44

Elephants, dolphins, and even some birds have lifelong friendships, just like humans!

Relationships with Teachers and Mentors

Great mentors and teachers inspire us to dream big and learn more. Here's why they're so impactful:

- **Favorite teachers**: Did you know that over 75% of students say they have at least one teacher who inspires them to do their best?

- **Extra help**: In the U.S., about 20% of students have a tutor or mentor to help with subjects like math or reading.

- **Staying connected**: After graduating, about 30% of people keep in touch with their favorite teacher!

- **Role models**: Kids with mentors are 50% more likely to do well in school and try new activities, like joining a club or playing sports.

- **Big brothers, big sisters**: This program helps over 250,000 kids every year by pairing them with a mentor to guide them.

Challenges and Support

Life's ups and downs are easier with people who care. Here's why support matters:

- **Sibling squabbles**: If you have brothers or sisters, you're not alone if you argue sometimes—about 60% of siblings fight at least once a week!

- **Talking it out**: Families that talk about their problems are 30% more likely to solve them quickly and stay close.

- **Chores**: Did you know that about 70% of kids help with chores like cleaning or cooking? Families that share chores are often happier and more organized.

- **Emotional support**: About 90% of kids say they feel better when they talk to their parents after a tough day.

Wacky Families

Every family has its quirks, and that's what makes them unique and fun! Here's why wacky families are the best:

- **Unique family pets**: About 20% of families in the U.S. have unusual pets like snakes, lizards, or even pet pigs!

- **Big families**: In some parts of the world, large families with 5 or more kids are still quite common! Did you know that the average family size in the U.S. is about 3.1 people, but in countries like India, it's more common to have 4 or 5 children?

- **Funny family names**: Over 1,000 people in the U.S. share the last name "Goofy"!

Fun Fact #45

Some families have super silly traditions, like wearing matching pajamas on vacations or eating dessert before dinner on special days!

Chapter 16: Languages and Linguistics

Have you ever wondered why people speak so many different languages? Or how words work together to create meaning? Welcome to the world of languages and linguistics! From counting how many languages there are to understanding how we learn to talk, let's explore some fascinating stats about the ways we communicate.

Languages Around the World

With thousands of languages spoken, the world is full of ways to connect and share. Here's why they're amazing:

- **Languages galore**: That's right—there are over 7,000 languages spoken in the world today.

- **Popular speaking**: The most popular language is English, spoken by about 1.5 billion people, but not everyone speaks it as their first language.

- **Many languages, small country**: Papua New Guinea, a small country, has the most languages in the world—over 800 different ones!

- **Endangered languages**: Every two weeks, a language disappears because fewer people use it. That's about 25 languages disappearing every year!

Fun Fact #46

In Welsh, there's a town called *Llanfairpwllgwyngyllgogerychwyrndro bwllllantysiliogogogoch!*

- **Language preservation**: Some endangered languages, like Hawaiian, are being saved with help from schools and kids learning to speak them again. Hawaiian language enrollment has grown by over 300% in the last two decades, with more than 13,000 students learning Hawaiian in schools today.

Learning Languages

Learning a new language opens doors to cultures, friends, and adventures. Here's why it's worth the effort:

- **First words**: Babies usually say their first word at around 12 months old, with "mama" or "dada" being the most common.

- **Brain power**: The part of the brain that helps with speaking and understanding words is called Broca's area. By age 3, most kids know about 1,000 words!

- **Bilingual kids**: These are people who speak two languages and they make up about 40% of people worldwide. Speaking two languages helps your brain! Studies show bilingual kids are better at solving puzzles and remembering things.

- **Fast learners**: Kids under the age of 10 can usually pick up a new language much faster than adults.

- **Innate learning**: Studies show that the average human can learn three to five languages during their lifetime!

- **Large languages**: After Mandarin Chinese, Spanish is the second most spoken language, with over 460 million speakers around the globe!

Languages in Everyday Life

From texting to talking, language is how we share ideas and express ourselves. Here's why it's so important:

- **Commonly used English word**: Did you know the most common word in English is "the," as people use it about 5% of the time when they speak or write.

- **Longggg words**: The longest word in the dictionary is pneumonoultramicroscopicsilicovolcanoconiosis, which has 45 letters! It's a type of lung disease.

- **Hands for communication**: Sign languages are used by about 70 million people around the world. They use hand movements, facial expressions, and body language to communicate.

- **Prevalence of sign language**: The most popular sign language is American Sign Language (ASL), used by about 500,000 people in the U.S. and Canada.

- **Deaf community**: Studies show that 90% of deaf individuals in the U.S. communicate primarily through sign language, and its unique grammar makes it a fully-fledged language, not just a translation of spoken English.

Fun Fact #47

In some parts of the world, people use whistles instead of words to communicate, like in the Canary Islands!

Language Fun Facts

Did you know some languages whistle instead of speak? Here are fun facts that show just how cool languages are:

- **Tongue twisters**: People love challenges like saying "She sells seashells by the seashore." In fact, the global market for word games, which includes tongue twisters, is expected to reach $19.2 billion by 2026.

- **Difficult tongue twisters**: The hardest tongue twister in English, according to scientists, is "Pad kid poured curd pulled cod." Studies show that it takes 3 times longer to say this tongue twister correctly compared to average sentences, due to its complex combination of consonants.

- **Words over the years**: New words are added to the dictionary all the time! In 2023, words like "bussin'" (meaning "really good") became official. Dictionaries add about 1,000 new words every year.

- **Emoji origin**: Did you know "emoji" is actually a Japanese word? It combines "e" (picture) and "moji" (character). About 10 billion emojis are sent every day!

Writing Systems

From hieroglyphs to alphabets, writing systems preserve history and ideas. Here's why they're fascinating:

- **Long alphabets**: The Khmer language in Cambodia has 74 letters—the longest alphabet in the world.

- **Short alphabets**: The alphabet for the Rotokas language (spoken in Papua New Guinea) has only 12 letters! Compare that to English, which has 26.

- **Origin of writing**: Around 4,000 years ago, people started using symbols to write. The first writing system was called cuneiform and looked like wedge-shaped marks.

- **Systems of writing**: Today, there are different writing systems like alphabets (like English), logograms (like Chinese), and syllabaries (like Japanese hiragana).

Languages and Technology

Apps and AI are helping preserve languages and teach them faster than ever. Here's how technology is changing the game:

- **Translation tools**: Have you ever used Google Translate? It can translate between 133 languages! Every day, people use it to translate about 100 billion words.

- **Translation fever**: The most translated website in the world is Wikipedia, available in 300+ languages.

Fun Fact #48

Games like Minecraft, Pokémon, and The Legend of Zelda have been translated into many languages, helping kids learn words without even realizing it!

- **Texting trends**: Did you know the average person sends about 94 text messages a day? That's over 34,000 texts a year!

- **Most used emoji**: Emojis are like a universal language. The most-used emoji is the laughing face with tears of joy!

Preserving and Sharing Languages

Saving endangered languages helps keep cultures alive. Here's why it's so important for the future:

- **Saving endangered languages**: There are about 2,500 languages around the world that are at risk of disappearing, and over 90% of these are spoken by fewer than 100,000 people.

- **Language learning growth**: More than 1 billion people worldwide are currently learning a new language, and Spanish and Mandarin Chinese are two of the most popular choices!

- **Digital language resources**: Over 200 languages are being taught online through apps and websites, helping kids and adults learn languages from the comfort of their homes.

- **Storytelling and language sharing**: In some countries, 50% of the population shares stories in their native language to help pass it down to younger generations.

Made-Up Languages

Made-up languages, or "conlangs," spark creativity and bring fictional worlds to life, from Elvish in Lord of the Rings to Klingon in Star Trek. Here are some fun facts that highlight their unique impact:

- **Languages in Movies**: Over 10 different made-up languages are used in the *Star Wars* movies, like the iconic Wookiee language, Shyriiwook, and Huttese, the language of Jabba the Hutt!

- **Klingon Speakers**: There are around 20,000 people worldwide who speak Klingon, the famous language from *Star Trek*. Some even translate books into Klingon, like *Shakespeare's Hamlet*!

Fun Fact #49

If you mix sounds, symbols, or words in a creative way, you can invent your own secret language just like authors!

- **Elvish Popularity**: Elvish, the language created by J.R.R. Tolkien for *The Lord of the Rings*, has over 1,000 words in its dictionary, and some fans have learned to speak it fluently.

- **Dothraki Fans**: The fictional language of Dothraki from *Game of Thrones* has over 3,000 words. It was created by linguist David J. Peterson, who made it for the show!

- **Invented for Fun**: Nearly 200 different made-up languages exist around the world, with fans creating their own languages for books, movies, and games, showing how creative people can be with words!

Chapter 17: Fashion and Design

Fashion isn't just about looking good—it's about telling a story, expressing creativity, and even helping the planet! Let's explore how fashion works, where it comes from, and why it's so much more than just clothes.

Understanding Fashion

Fashion is more than clothes—it's a way to express who you are! Here are some key stats that show why it's so important:

- **What is fashion**: Fashion is how people express themselves through clothes, shoes, and accessories. Did you know that people spend an average of $1.5 trillion every year on fashion worldwide?

- **Outfit mayhem**: Over 7 billion outfits are worn every day—one for every person on Earth!

- **Styles of clothing**: There are different styles, like casual, formal, sporty, and cultural. About 60% of kids say their favorite style is casual, like T-shirts and jeans.

- **Shoe variety**: Shoes are a big part of style too. The average person owns about 19 pairs of shoes, but many kids love their sneakers the most!

The History of Fashion

Fashion tells the story of the past, from ancient robes to modern streetwear. Here are some highlights from its fascinating journey through time:

- **Early clothing**: Humans started wearing clothes about 170,000 years ago, using animal skins to keep warm.

- **Designer clothes**: The first "designer" clothes appeared in Ancient Egypt. Pharaohs wore special robes decorated with gold and jewels, and the Egyptians invented linen, one of the first fabrics.

- **Fashion through the ages**: The Middle Ages brought colorful robes and fancy hats, but it wasn't until the 1800s that clothes were made in factories.

- **Jean frenzy**: The invention of denim jeans in 1873 changed everything. Today, over 1.25 billion pairs of jeans are sold every year!

Fashion Around the World

Fashion is as diverse as the people who wear it! Explore how cultures worldwide use style to celebrate their identity:

- **Scottish traditional clothing**: Scotland is known for its kilts, a knee-length skirt for men. They've been around for over 400 years!

- **Indian traditional clothing**: In India, over 300 million women wear a traditional outfit called the sari for celebrations.

- **Japanese traditional clothing**: In Japan, the kimono is worn for special occasions. About 20 million people in Japan still wear them for festivals and weddings.

- **Cultural colors**: In China, red is a lucky color, so many people wear red during the Lunar New Year, celebrated by 1.4 billion people worldwide.

- **Brides around the world**: In Western countries, most dresses worn by brides are white, but in India, most brides wear red or gold for their wedding ceremonies.

How Fashion is Made

Ever wonder how your favorite outfits come to life? From design to runway, here's a look at how fashion is created:

- **From idea to outfit**: Designers sketch about 50 ideas for every outfit, but only a few get made.

- **Cash crop**: Cotton is the most-used material in the world, with over 25 million tons grown each year.

Fun Fact #50

In the past, only wealthy people could afford glasses, but now they're a cool fashion statement for everyone.

- **Clothing factories**: Most clothes are made in factories. It takes about 2 weeks to make a simple T-shirt but up to 6 months for fancy dresses!

- **New materials**: Scientists are creating eco-friendly fabrics, like cloth made from pineapple leaves or recycled plastic bottles. Every year, over 1 billion T-shirts are made from recycled materials.

Fashion Trends

Trends come and go, but they shape how we dress and express ourselves. Check out the stats behind what's in and what's out:

- **Trending styles**: Every year, new styles become popular. Did you know that social media helps spread trends to over 4 billion people?

- **Popular footwear**: Sneakers are the most popular type of shoe, with over 1.5 billion pairs sold each year!

- **Expressive shirts**: About 70% of kids say they love wearing graphic T-shirts with their favorite characters or designs.

- **How trends start**: Celebrities have a huge impact on fashion. When a famous singer or actor wears something cool, sales for that item often increase by 300% in just one week!

Sustainability in Fashion

Fashion can be fun and eco-friendly! Learn how the industry is working to protect the planet, one outfit at a time:

- **Clothing waste**: About 92 million tons of clothes are thrown away every year. That's like dumping a garbage truck full of clothes every second!

- **Reducing waste**: Recycling clothes helps the planet. For example, 1 recycled T-shirt saves about 700 gallons of water.

- **Thrift shopping**: More people are buying second-hand clothes to save money and reduce waste. Around 42% of people now shop at thrift stores or online resale sites.

Fashion Fun Facts

Did you know the first sunglasses were invented to block out Arctic glare? Here are some more fun facts about the world of fashion:

- **Big shirts**: The largest T-shirt ever made was 300 feet wide and weighed over 5,000 pounds. It could fit a whole school of kids inside!

Fun Fact #51

When zippers were first invented, they were only used on boots and fancy purses—not clothes!

- **Expensive footwear**: The world's most expensive shoes are diamond-encrusted heels that cost $17 million.

- **Outfit variety**: On average, kids wear about 7 different outfits every week, but their favorite outfit gets worn 3 times more than others.

- **Storing style**: Backpacks are a popular accessory too. Over 25 million backpacks are sold each year in the U.S.

The Future of Fashion

From high-tech fabrics to virtual fashion shows, the future of fashion is bold and exciting. Here's a glimpse of what's next:

- **Futuristic clothing**: Smart clothes are on the rise! Imagine wearing a jacket that can charge your phone or a shirt that changes color with your mood. Over 10 million smart clothing items are sold each year.

- **3D printed clothes**: One day, you might 3D print your favorite shoes or outfits at home. Experts say this could happen in the next 20 years.

- **AI and graphic design**: Artificial intelligence (AI) is helping designers make new looks faster. By 2030, 30% of designs could be created using AI tools.

Chapter 18: Food and Culinary Arts

Food is amazing—it keeps us strong, brings people together, and can be incredibly fun to make and eat. From juicy burgers to colorful sushi, every meal has a story and even some surprising numbers behind it. Let's dig in and learn some tasty facts about food and cooking!

The World of Food

Food isn't just fuel—it's culture, comfort, and creativity on a plate! Here are some stats that highlight why food brings us all together:

- **Pasta, pasta, pasta**: There are over 250 types of pasta around the world, from spaghetti to macaroni!

- **Eating a ton**: Around 7.9 billion meals are eaten every single day on Earth. That's one meal for every person alive!

- **Pizza craze**: In the U.S., pizza is a top favorite. Americans eat about 3 billion pizzas every year—that's 46 slices per person!

- **Sushi galore**: In Japan, sushi is a popular dish. Over 5 million sushi rolls are sold daily in Tokyo alone.

- **Spice-filled cuisine**: India is known for spicy curries, and about 70% of Indian households use spices like turmeric and cumin every day in their cooking.

Fun Fact #52

The first pizzas in Italy were flatbreads with toppings, and some were even square-shaped!

The History of Cooking

From fire-roasted meals to high-tech kitchens, cooking has an amazing history. Here's a taste of how it all started:

- **Origin of cooking**: Cooking started over 1.5 million years ago when humans learned to control fire. Roasting meat was one of the first cooking techniques.

- **Ancient food**: Bread is one of the oldest foods. The first loaf was made over 14,000 years ago, and now, 90 billion loaves are baked every year!

- **Famous food invention**: The chocolate chip cookie was invented in 1938. Today, about 7 billion cookies are eaten annually in the U.S. alone.

- **Cold served goodness**: Ice cream has been around for over 2,000 years, and the most popular flavor is vanilla, chosen by 59% of people in surveys.

Cooking Fun Facts

Did you know popcorn was discovered over 5,000 years ago? Here are more fun tidbits about the magic of cooking:

- **Quick and easy**: Did you know it takes just 10 minutes to cook a bowl of instant noodles? Around 290 million servings of noodles are eaten every day worldwide.

- **Simple and filling**: Sandwiches are a quick favorite, with 300 million sandwiches eaten daily in the U.S.

- **Big breakfast**: The largest pancake ever made was over 49 feet wide—big enough for an entire playground of kids!

- **Many slices of joy**: The longest pizza stretched 1.2 miles and took over 23 hours to make. It had enough slices for 30,000 people!

Exploring Flavors

Sweet, salty, sour, bitter—flavors make food exciting! Discover how exploring them can transform any dish:

- **Variety of tastes**: Did you know your tongue can detect at least 5 different flavors? Sweet, salty, sour, bitter, and umami (a savory taste).

- **Kid superpower**: Kids have more taste buds than adults, which is why about 50% of kids prefer sweeter foods, like chocolate or fruit.

- **Spicy pepper**: One of the world's spiciest peppers, the Carolina Reaper, measures over 2 million Scoville units, the scale used to measure heat. That's about 500 times spicier than a jalapeño!

Fun Fact #53

Before people added sugar, ancient Mayans and Aztecs drank chocolate as a spicy, bitter drink instead of a sweet treat!

- **Enjoyment of spice**: In Mexico, about 85% of people enjoy spicy foods, often adding chili to tacos, sauces, and snacks.

How Food is Made

From farm to fork, food goes on quite the journey. Here's a peek at how your favorite meals come to life:

- **Farming frenzy**: Many of the foods we eat come from farms. For example, the U.S. produces over 900 million pounds of strawberries every year. That's a lot of berry desserts!

- **Dairy demand**: Milk is another big favorite. Cows produce about 6.3 gallons of milk per day—enough for a lot of bowls of cereal.

- **Factory-made foods**: Some foods, like chips and cookies, are made in factories. Did you know over 16 billion bags of chips are sold each year worldwide?

- **Fresh foods**: However, fresh fruits and vegetables are still super popular. Bananas are the world's most eaten fruit, with more than 100 billion bananas consumed every year.

Culinary Arts and Creativity

Cooking is art you can eat! From plating to new recipes, here's how chefs use creativity to make every meal special:

- **Food art**: Some chefs create amazing food art that turns meals into masterpieces! Did you know that the global cake decorating market is valued at over $1.1 billion and growing? And in food competitions, cakes can weigh up to 1,000 pounds and stand as tall as 4 feet!

- **Decoration fun**: Did you know that about 40% of kids say their favorite part of cooking is decorating cupcakes or cookies?

- **Culinary kids**: Cooking isn't just for grown-ups. Over 60% of kids ages 6-12 help out in the kitchen at least once a week.

- **Baking fun**: Baking is a top pick for young chefs, with chocolate chip cookies being the most common treat made at home.

> ### Fun Fact #54
>
> Chefs can use super cold liquid nitrogen to make ice cream freeze instantly—it even creates a cool fog effect!

Healthy Eating

Eating healthy fuels your body and mind, keeping you strong and happy. Check out why nutrition is so important:

- **Variety and health**: Eating a mix of foods is important. Nutrition experts recommend filling 50% of your plate with fruits and veggies at every meal.

- **Top veggie**: Carrots are a top veggie for kids, with over 2 billion pounds eaten each year in the U.S.

- **Apple variety**: Apples are super healthy and come in over 7,500 varieties. Granny Smith apples are known to be the tartest!

- **H2O necessity**: Water is also key—about 60% of your body is made up of water, and you should drink about 8 cups a day to stay hydrated.

Food Around the World

Every culture has its own delicious dishes. Explore how food connects us, no matter where we're from:

- **Food festivities**: Thailand celebrates a Monkey Buffet Festival where over 2 tons of fruits and veggies are served to monkeys each year!

- **Tomato battle**: In Spain, the Tomatina festival features a giant tomato fight, using over 145,000 pounds of tomatoes.

- **Street food wonder**: Street food is super popular. In China, over 115 million people eat street food every day, enjoying items like dumplings and skewers.

- **NYC staple**: In New York City, hot dogs are a classic street food. About 20 million hot dogs are sold from street carts every year.

The Future of Food

What's next in food? Think lab-grown meat, eco-friendly packaging, and more. Here's a bite of what's coming:

- **Lab foods**: Scientists are creating new foods, like lab-grown burgers, which use 90% less water and land than traditional beef.

- **Bugging out**: Bug-based snacks are becoming more common, with over 2 billion people worldwide already eating insects as a source of protein.

- **Robo cooks**: Robot chefs are being tested in some restaurants. By 2030, experts say robots could make up to 25% of restaurant meals!

- **Printed food**: 3D-printed food is also on the rise. Imagine printing a pizza at the touch of a button.

Fun Fact #55

Tiny plants like spirulina are packed with nutrients and might become a common ingredient in future smoothies and snacks!

Chapter 19: Mythology and Legends

Have you ever wondered about the amazing stories people have told for thousands of years? Mythology and legends are packed with gods, heroes, and magical creatures. These tales aren't just entertaining— they also tell us about history, culture, and even how people explained the world before science. Let's explore the numbers behind these epic stories!

Popular Myths Around the World

Myths bring magic to life! They're full of tales that inspire, teach, and connect cultures everywhere. Here's why they're unforgettable:

- **The most famous gods**: Zeus, the king of the Greek gods, appears in over 60% of Greek myths that have been studied. That's a lot of thunderbolts!

- **Heroic adventures**: The story of Hercules has been retold in over 25 different languages and even inspired movies and TV shows watched by millions.

- **Olympus tales**: Over 100 myths are connected to Mount Olympus, the legendary home of the Greek gods.

- **Ragnarök stories**: About 30% of Norse legends involve Ragnarök, the end-of-the-world tale where gods and monsters clash in an epic battle.

- **Viking favorites**: Thor, the god of thunder, is the most recognized Norse god today, thanks to his appearances in movies. Surveys show that 85% of people who know Norse mythology recognize Thor before any other god.

- **India's epics**: The "Mahabharata" and "Ramayana" are two of the longest epic poems in the world. Together, they total more than 200,000 verses—that's like reading a stack of books taller than you!

- **Chinese dragons**: Over 70% of Chinese legends feature dragons as symbols of power, strength, and good luck.

Magical Creatures and Beasts

From fire-breathing dragons to mysterious unicorns, magical creatures spark our imagination. Check out the legends behind these fascinating beings:

- **Mermaid myths**: Over 60% of coastal cultures have legends about mermaids, from the sirens in tales from Greek mythology to the selkies in Scottish folklore.

- **Friendly or scary**: While 80% of European dragon stories describe them as dangerous, in Asia, dragons are considered wise and helpful in more than 90% of legends.

Fun Fact #56

In old stories, fairies loved playing pranks on people, like hiding their shoes or making them dance all night!

- **Unicorn sightings**: Tales of unicorns have been told for over 2,000 years! In the Middle Ages, unicorns were so popular that nearly every royal family in Europe included unicorns in their crests or symbols.

- **Global dragons**: There are stories about dragons that appear in over 45 different cultures worldwide. They come from all over, from Europe to Asia, almost every ancient society imagined these fantastic creatures.

How Myths Explained the World

Before science, myths helped people understand the mysteries of life, from thunder to the stars. Here's how these stories shaped ancient beliefs:

- **Stormy gods**: About 40% of ancient myths use gods to explain weather events. For example, in Greek mythology, Zeus controls thunder, while in Norse tales, Thor brings storms with his hammer.

- **Constellations, myths, and more**: Over 80% of constellations are linked to myths. For example, the constellation of Orion represents a hunter from Greek mythology, while the Big Dipper is part of a bear legend for Native American tribes.

- **Volcanoes and mountains**: Myths about volcanoes are common in over 20 different cultures. Hawaiians told stories about Pele, the goddess of fire, while Romans believed Vulcan forged weapons under fiery mountains.

- **Eclipses**: In ancient China, people thought a dragon was eating the sun during a solar eclipse. Over 70% of ancient eclipse myths included creatures swallowing the sun or moon.

Heroes and Their Stories

Every hero has a journey! Myths are packed with brave warriors and clever tricksters whose adventures still captivate us today:

- **Across the globe**: Researchers found that 90% of cultures have stories about heroes who face challenges, gain wisdom, and save the day. This pattern is called "The Hero's Journey."

- **Longest journey**: Odysseus from Greek mythology spent 10 years traveling home in the famous story "The Odyssey."

- **Strong women**: Don't forget the heroines! Legends like Mulan from China and Amaterasu from Japan show that bravery isn't just for boys. Surveys reveal that 55% of kids today say they're inspired by female heroes in myths.

Myths and Legends in Modern Times

Myths aren't just ancient history—they're alive in books, movies, and even video games! Discover how these timeless tales continue to inspire us:

- **Books and movies**: Myths inspire so many stories today! Over 75% of superhero movies, like those about Thor or Wonder Woman, are based on ancient myths and legends.

- **Names we use**: More than 50 moons in our solar system are named after characters from myths, like Europa (from Greek myths) and Titan (from Norse stories).

- **Festivals for myths**: In Japan, the Shinto creation myth is celebrated every year during festivals like Setsubun. About 60% of Japanese families take part in these events to honor their legends.

- **Mythology classes**: In the U.S., about 30% of schools include mythology as part of their curriculum. Kids love learning about the exciting adventures of gods, heroes, and creatures!

Fun Fact #57

While zombies aren't real, some legends say certain old medicines and potions could make people act like them.

Chapter 20: Adventure and Exploration

Exploration is all about discovering new places, climbing to the tops of mountains, diving deep into the ocean, or traveling to faraway lands. Adventure has always been part of human history, and there's a lot we can learn from those who dared to go where no one else had been. Let's dive into the numbers behind some of the greatest adventures and explorations ever!

Exploring New Lands

Exploration has shaped our world, from uncovering hidden treasures to discovering new cultures. Here's why the spirit of adventure still matters today:

- **Christopher Columbus**: Columbus sailed across the Atlantic Ocean in 1492 with a crew of about 90 men on three ships. His voyages are often credited with connecting Europe and the Americas, leading to massive changes in history.

- **Ferdinand Magellan**: Magellan's expedition was the first to sail all the way around the world. It took three years (1519–1522), and out of the original 270 sailors, only 18 survived the journey.

Fun Fact #58

Scientists called astronaut analogs live in remote places like deserts or underwater to test what space travel might be like!

- **Polar explorers**: Ernest Shackleton led expeditions to Antarctica in the early 1900s. During one trip, his ship, the *Endurance*, got stuck in ice for over 10 months, but all 28 crew members survived thanks to Shackleton's leadership.

- **Mount Everest climbers**: Since the first recorded summit in 1953, over 6,000 people have reached the top of Mount Everest, the tallest mountain in the world. However, the journey is tough—about 4% of climbers don't make it back safely.

Oceans and Deep-Sea Adventures

The ocean is a mysterious, watery world full of secrets. From shipwrecks to strange sea creatures, here's why deep-sea exploration is so important:

- **The HMS Beagle**: In the 1830s, this British ship carried Charles Darwin, who studied animals and plants on the Galápagos Islands. His observations helped him develop the theory of evolution. The voyage lasted five years and covered over 40,000 miles!

- **The Titanic**: The *Titanic* sank in 1912, but its wreck wasn't found until 1985. Scientists had to search an area of about 200 square miles at a depth of 12,500 feet to locate it.

- **The Mariana Trench**: The Mariana Trench in the Pacific Ocean is the deepest part of the world's oceans, going down nearly 7 miles. Only 3 people have ever gone to the very bottom, fewer than the number of people who have walked on the Moon!

- **Jacques Cousteau's discoveries**: Jacques Cousteau, a famous underwater explorer, helped invent scuba diving equipment in the 1940s. Thanks to his work, over 11 million people around the world are certified scuba divers today.

Outer Space: The Final Frontier

Space is the ultimate adventure! From landing on the Moon to searching for life on Mars, here are the big reasons we're reaching for the stars:

- **The first satellite**: In 1957, the Soviet Union launched *Sputnik*, the first satellite, into space. It weighed just 184 pounds, about the same as a large dog.

- **Searching for life**: Scientists believe that planets like Europa (a moon of Jupiter) could have life because it has an icy surface and possibly an ocean underneath. Over 40 spacecrafts have been sent to study Jupiter and its moons.

- **International Space Station (ISS)**: The ISS has been in orbit around Earth since 1998. Astronauts from around 19 different countries have lived and worked there, conducting over 3,300 experiments in zero gravity.

Fun Fact #59

Depending on how hot they are, stars can be red, yellow, white, or even blue! Blue stars are the hottest, while red stars are the coolest (but still really hot!).

- **The Moon landing**: The Apollo 11 mission with Neil Armstrong lasted 8 days, and over 600 million people around the world watched it live on TV.

- **Mars rovers**: NASA's rover *Curiosity* has been exploring Mars since 2012. It has traveled over 17 miles and sent back more than 500,000 photos of the red planet.

Adventures in Science

Science is like a never-ending treasure hunt, unlocking mysteries about our planet, health, and the universe. Here's why it's worth exploring:

- **Rainforests**: Scientists estimate that there are about 10 million species of plants and animals on Earth, but we've only discovered about 20% of them. Rainforests are one of the best places to find new species—more than 400 new species have been discovered in the Amazon rainforest since 2010.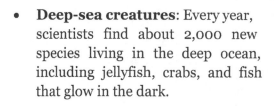

- **Deep-sea creatures**: Every year, scientists find about 2,000 new species living in the deep ocean, including jellyfish, crabs, and fish that glow in the dark.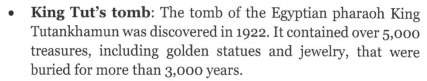

- **King Tut's tomb**: The tomb of the Egyptian pharaoh King Tutankhamun was discovered in 1922. It contained over 5,000 treasures, including golden statues and jewelry, that were buried for more than 3,000 years.

- **Lost cities**: Using satellite technology, archaeologists have found more than 4,000 ancient cities in regions like Central America. These include Mayan cities hidden in dense jungles.

How We Explore Today

From drones to submarines to spaceships, modern technology makes exploration more exciting than ever. Here's how we're exploring new frontiers:

- **Drones**: Scientists use drones to map forests, track wildlife, and even explore volcanoes. Drones can reach places too dangerous for humans, and their use has increased by 300% over the past decade.

- **Climbing and hiking**: Each year, more than 50 million people visit national parks in the U.S. to hike, climb, and explore nature.

> **Fun Fact #60**
>
> Future spaceships might travel at warp speed or use ion engines, making trips to faraway planets much faster!

- **Space tourism**: In 2021, the first all-civilian crew went to space for three days. Companies like SpaceX plan to take tourists to space regularly, with tickets costing around $55 million per person!

Chapter 21: Crafts and DIY Projects

Crafts and DIY (Do-It-Yourself) projects are amazing ways to use your imagination, build things, and have fun while learning new skills. Whether it's making a bracelet, building a birdhouse, or designing a robot, creating something with your own hands feels great! Let's explore the numbers behind crafting and DIY around the world.

The Popularity of Crafting

Crafting is more than a hobby—it's a creative escape that millions of people love! Here are some stats that show just how popular it's become:

- **Sewing and knitting**: In recent years, sewing and knitting have made a comeback, with more than 1 in 3 families trying these crafts at home. Kids especially enjoy making small stuffed animals or scarves.

- **Crafting communities**: In the U.S., about 63% of households participate in some form of crafting or DIY each year. That means nearly 82 million families enjoy making things together!

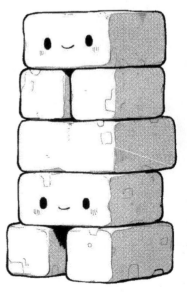

- **Drawing and painting**: Among kids, drawing and painting are the top crafting activities, with about 8 out of 10 kids saying they've made art with crayons, markers, or paint.

- **Young crafters**: Kids love crafting too! Surveys show that 70% of children ages 6-12 have done a craft project in school or at home in the past year.

- **Global crafting**: Around the world, people spend over $43 billion on craft supplies annually. That's enough to buy about 86 million bicycles!

Craft Supplies: The Numbers Add Up

From colorful yarn to glitter galore, craft supplies fuel imagination. Here's a fun look at the numbers behind these DIY must-haves:

- **Paper and glue**: Every year, people in the U.S. use about 10 million gallons of glue for arts and crafts. If you poured all that glue into swimming pools, it would fill 15 Olympic-sized pools!

- **Yarn**: Yarn is super popular for knitting and crochet. Americans buy enough yarn each year to wrap around the Earth about 70 times.

- **Recycled materials**: Nearly 25% of craft projects use recycled materials like old boxes, bottle caps, or newspapers. This helps reduce waste while encouraging creativity!

Fun Fact #61

Some crafters use extra-large knitting needles to make huge, fluffy blankets in no time!

- **Saving the planet**: Crafting with recycled or natural materials is a growing trend. About 60% of crafters say they've made at least one eco-friendly project, like turning old jars into lanterns or making tote bags from old T-shirts.

DIY Projects for the Home

DIY projects turn ordinary spaces into something special. Check out why crafting your own décor is all the rage:

- **Handmade furniture**: In the U.S., more than 15 million people have built their own furniture, like bookshelves or tables. DIY furniture saves families an average of $200 per piece compared to buying from a store.

- **Room makeovers**: About 40% of homeowners say they've done at least one DIY room makeover, such as painting walls or putting up shelves. Painting is the most popular project, with people using enough paint each year to cover over 2 billion square feet—that's like painting 35,000 football fields!

- **Birdhouses and feeders**: More than 20% of families in the U.S. have built a birdhouse or bird feeder as a DIY project. This helps birds, especially during winter months.

- **Garden decor**: Kids and adults alike love decorating gardens. Every year, people make about 7 million handmade garden ornaments, like painted rocks or wind chimes.

The Benefits of Crafting

Crafting isn't just fun—it's good for you! From reducing stress to boosting happiness, here are the perks of getting crafty:

- **Boosting creativity**: Studies show that kids who do crafts are 73% more likely to think of creative solutions to problems than kids who don't.

- **Stress relief**: Research shows that 81% of people feel calmer and happier after spending time on a craft project. Even just 20 minutes of crafting can reduce stress levels by up to 25%!

- **Building connections**: Family crafting time is great for bonding. About 3 in 5 families say they feel closer after working on a project together, whether it's baking, building, or creating art.

Crafts Around the World

Every culture has unique crafts that tell its story. Discover the amazing traditions and techniques from around the globe:

- **Origami in Japan**: Origami, the art of paper folding, is practiced by millions of people in Japan and around the world. On International Origami Day, over 10 million paper cranes are folded and shared to promote peace.

- **Weaving in Africa**: In countries like Ghana, traditional Kente cloth is handwoven using colorful threads. Each design tells a story, and some patterns have been used for over 400 years.

- **Maker culture**: The maker movement is a global trend where people use technology and tools to create everything from robots to handmade jewelry. There are more than 2,000 maker fairs held worldwide every year, attracting millions of visitors who want to learn and create.

- **Online crafting communities**: Platforms like YouTube and Pinterest have made crafting more popular than ever. Over 30 million crafting tutorials are available online, helping people learn new skills and share their projects.

Fun Fact #62

Aboriginal artists in Australia create dot paintings, using tiny dots of paint to form incredible patterns and images that tell stories about nature and history!

Chapter 22: Aviation and Aerospace

Flying through the skies and exploring outer space might seem like something out of a dream, but it's real life! Aviation (flying planes) and aerospace (space exploration) are all about adventure, technology, and discovery. Let's dive into the world of planes, rockets, and space travel and uncover the amazing statistics behind it all.

The History of Flight

From the Wright brothers to supersonic jets, the history of flight is a story of bold dreams and incredible innovation. Here are some highlights that show how it all began:

- **Prevalence of flight**: Today, over 4 billion people fly on airplanes every year. That's more than half of the world's population traveling through the air!

- **Growth of aviation**: The aviation industry has grown a lot since then, with over 100,000 flights taking off and landing around the world every day!

- **Golden age of aviation**: Airplanes became faster and more advanced in the 20th century. By the 1950s, commercial airlines could carry more passengers. In 1958, the Boeing 707 was introduced, and it could hold up to 181 passengers at once.

- **Things done Wright**: Humans have dreamed of flying for thousands of years, but it wasn't until 1903 that the Wright brothers built the first successful airplane. That flight lasted just 12 seconds and covered 120 feet, about the length of a basketball court.

Modern Aviation

Today's aviation connects the world like never before, making travel faster, safer, and more accessible. Check out the stats that make modern flight amazing:

- **How planes work**: Planes can fly because of something called "lift." Air moves over the wings in a way that helps keep the plane up in the sky. A typical passenger jet flies at a speed of 550 miles per hour, which is about 10 times faster than a car on the highway.

- **Flying large**: The largest passenger plane in the world, the Airbus A380, can carry over 850 people at one time. That's like flying an entire school in one plane!

Fun Fact #63

Commercial airplanes use autopilot for most of the flight, meaning computers help fly the plane while pilots monitor everything!

- **Irrational fear**: Flying is actually one of the safest ways to travel. Statistics show that the chances of being in a plane accident are about 1 in 11 million, which is much safer than driving a car.

- **Prepared pilots**: Pilots go through thousands of hours of training to make sure they're prepared. On average, a commercial pilot has completed over 1,500 hours of flight training before flying a big passenger plane.

The New Frontier of Space

Space isn't just for astronauts anymore! From satellites to space tourism, here's why exploring the final frontier is more exciting than ever:

- **Rare travels**: Since Neil Armstrong's landing on the moon in 1969, there has only been 12 astronauts who have walked on the moon.

- **Costly travel**: Space missions are incredibly expensive. The Apollo program cost about $25 billion in the 1960s, which would be over $150 billion in today's money.

- **Moon bases**: Plans for a permanent moon base are underway! Scientists estimate that by 2040, astronauts could live and work on the moon for up to 6 months at a time.

- **Space jobs for kids today**: Did you know there are over 18,000 people working for NASA right now? By the time today's kids grow up, the number of space jobs could double with more private companies joining in.

- **Reusable rockets**: SpaceX is making rockets reusable, lowering costs and making space travel more frequent. A Falcon 9 rocket can now be reused up to 15 times, saving millions of dollars with each launch.

The Technology of Flight

Flight technology is a mix of science and magic (okay, mostly science). Discover how cutting-edge tech keeps planes soaring high:

- **Fuel saving**: Modern airplanes are much more fuel-efficient than they used to be. For example, today's planes use about 80% less fuel per passenger than planes in the 1960s.

- **Widespread drone usage**: Drones, which are small unmanned flying machines, are becoming more common. It's estimated that there are over 1.1 million drones registered in the United States alone!

- **Faster than a speeding bullet**: The fastest jet, the SR-71 Blackbird, can fly at 2,193 miles per hour. That's over three times the speed of sound and faster than a bullet!

Fun Fact #64

Unlike regular airplanes, helicopters can hover in place, fly sideways, and even go backward!

- **Tiny but mighty**: The smallest drone ever made, called the "Black Hornet," is about the size of a paperclip and weighs only 18 grams, but it can fly up to 25 minutes and is used for important missions.

- **Planes on the Internet**: At any moment, there are about 9,728 airplanes flying in the sky worldwide, tracked in real-time by websites like Flightradar24.

- **Building a giant**: It took over 3.5 million parts to assemble the Boeing 747, one of the world's largest and most famous airplanes.

- **Heavy into space**: Rockets are used to send astronauts and satellites into space. A rocket like the SpaceX Falcon 9 can carry up to 50,000 pounds of cargo into orbit. That's like sending five elephants into space!

The Future of Aviation and Aerospace

Think flying taxis and zero-emission planes—aviation's future is straight out of a sci-fi movie. Here are some stats that make it real:

- **Electric planes**: Airplanes are becoming more eco-friendly. Engineers are working on electric planes that produce no emissions. By 2040, it's estimated that about 25% of planes could be powered by electricity.

- **Emission reduction**: Sustainable fuels made from plants or recycled materials are also being used. These fuels could reduce airplane emissions by up to 80%.

- **Futuristic travel**: By 2040, there could be over 430,000 flying cars zooming through the skies. Companies like Uber and others are already testing them!

- **Sonic the airplane**: New supersonic planes, like the Boom Overture, could fly at speeds of over 1,300 miles per hour, cutting travel time in half. By 2029, passengers might be flying from New York to London in just 3.5 hours!

- **Solar power**: Solar planes like Solar Impulse have already flown around the world using only the sun! By 2050, 20% of planes might use solar energy for power.

- **New industry**: Scientists predict that by 2050, we might mine asteroids for metals like gold and platinum. Some asteroids could be worth over $1 trillion!

Fun Fact #65

Some future planes might replace regular windows with VR screens, letting you pick any view you want. This would also come with the option to see the natural views instead.

Chapter 23: Personal Development and Success

Everyone wants to grow and succeed, but what does that mean? Personal development is about learning new skills, growing as a person, and setting goals to become the best version of yourself. Success can look different for everyone—it could mean winning a race, making a new friend, or building something amazing. Let's look at how people develop and succeed through numbers and facts!

Setting Goals

Setting goals is like creating a map for your dreams—it helps you stay focused and get where you want to go. Here's why goals matter:

- **Better results**: Studies show that people who write down their goals are 42% more likely to achieve them. For kids, this could mean writing down goals like reading a new book or practicing a sport!

- **Big goals take time**: Research says it takes about 66 days to form a new habit, like practicing piano daily or brushing your teeth without being reminded.

- **Start young**: Kids who set small, daily goals often perform better in school. About 88% of kids who use goal-setting tools say it helps them focus and feel proud when they achieve their goals.

- **Step by step**: Breaking big goals into smaller steps makes them easier to reach. For example, if you want to run a mile, you might start by jogging for 5 minutes every day.

- **Success rate**: Around 76% of people say they reach their goals when they make a detailed plan for how to achieve them.

Learning and Growing

Every mistake is a chance to learn, and every step forward helps you grow. Here are some stats that show why personal growth is so powerful:

- **Learning matters**: People who continue learning after school are happier and earn more money. For adults, getting more education can increase income by up to 10% per year! For kids, every new thing you learn builds your skills for the future.

- **Teamwork wins**: About 80% of people say they solve problems faster when they work with others, like on group projects or team sports.

Fun Fact #66

Writing down goals makes them real! If you write your goals down, it's like telling your brain, "This is what I want to do," and it makes it easier to stay focused!

- **Practice makes perfect**: Did you know it takes about 10,000 hours of practice to become really good at something, like playing violin or becoming a great artist? That's about 3 hours a day for 10 years!

- **Reading for success**: Kids who read for fun at least 20 minutes a day score better in school and know about 1.8 million more words by the time they finish high school than kids who don't.

- **Creative minds**: Kids who do creative activities, like drawing or building, are 70% more likely to come up with unique ideas to solve problems.

Staying Positive

A positive attitude can turn challenges into opportunities. Check out why staying positive is a game-changer for success:

- **Positive thinking**: Kids who stay positive about challenges are more likely to keep trying until they succeed. Studies show that about 75% of people who think positively feel more motivated to reach their goals.

- **Don't give up**: It's normal to face setbacks. About 85% of successful people say they failed at something before they succeeded. For example, Walt Disney was told he lacked creativity before creating Disneyland!

- **Asking for help**: People who ask for help from teachers, friends, or family when they're stuck are 4 times more likely to find solutions faster.

- **Confidence counts**: People with high self-confidence are 31% more likely to try new things, like learning a new skill or making friends.

Healthy Habits for Success

Good habits, like eating well and staying active, are the building blocks of a happy and successful life. Here's why they're so important:

- **Brains love exercise**: Kids who stay active for at least 60 minutes a day have better focus in school and perform up to 20% better on tests.

- **Team sports help**: Playing sports can improve leadership skills. About 73% of CEOs who lead big companies played team sports when they were younger.

- **Sleep is super important**: Kids who get at least 9-11 hours of sleep each night are healthier and perform up to 30% better in school.

- **Sleep and mood**: Getting enough rest helps people feel happier—studies show that kids who don't sleep enough are 3 times more likely to feel stressed.

Celebrating Success

Big or small, every win deserves a celebration! Recognizing your achievements keeps you motivated for the next adventure:

- **One step at a time**: Celebrating small achievements, like learning how to tie your shoes or acing a spelling test, boosts happiness by up to 25%, making you more likely to keep going!

- **Cheering each other on**: People who celebrate their friends' or teammates' successes feel 50% more connected to others, which helps build stronger friendships.

- **Having fun**: About 87% of kids say they enjoy working toward a goal more when it feels fun, like turning homework into a game or doing chores with music playing.

Fun Fact #67

You don't need a huge party to celebrate—dancing around, eating your favorite treat, or telling someone you're proud of yourself all count as celebrations!

Conclusion: The Power of Yourself and Knowledge

We've been on an incredible journey through numbers, facts, and stats that show how amazing our world is. From learning about animals and education to exploring history, sports, and inventions, we've uncovered so many cool things! Let's look back at what we've learned and think about how numbers can help us understand and change the world.

The Future of Innovation

Numbers tell incredible stories, and they help us understand the world better. Did you know that people remember facts 22% better when they're linked to numbers? By reading this book, you've connected amazing stats to fascinating topics, from animals and the environment to sports and space. On average, kids your age learn something new every 10 minutes during school, and now you've learned even more outside the classroom! But the journey doesn't stop here—share your favorite fact with a friend, because about 90% of people enjoy teaching others something new.

You also have the power to make a difference. Remember, 25% of the Earth's species are at risk of extinction, but small actions like recycling or planting trees can help save them. Education changes lives too—though 260 million kids worldwide can't attend school, programs are helping millions more learn and thrive. Even planting a single tree can make a difference, cleaning up the air by absorbing 48 pounds of carbon dioxide every year.

Dreaming big can change the world. By 2030, 20 million new jobs in coding, space exploration, and renewable energy will need curious thinkers like you. NASA is planning trips to Mars—what do you think life on another planet would look like? And don't forget the power of teamwork—75% of kids who play team sports say it helps them make friends. Whether you're working on an invention, exploring new places, or helping a team, big dreams can lead to amazing futures.

Finally, remember that even small steps make a difference. Ask questions—kids ask about 300 every day, and that curiosity leads to growth. Help others with little actions, like sharing, volunteering, or picking up litter—it can make you 24% happier! And don't forget to set goals—writing them down makes you 42% more likely to achieve them. What will you learn, share, and accomplish next? The world is waiting for your ideas and actions—so go out there and make it a better place!

Thanks + Freebies!

I hope you enjoyed this book! As a small indie publisher, it means a TON to me that you read all the way to this point, and I hope I have made a difference in your pursuit of knowledge in a positive way!

As thanks for purchasing this book, you now have access to a wide array of bonus materials that will provide hours of fun and enjoyment alongside an email list where we provide even more goodies, such as coloring pages and activity sheets weekly, at no extra cost! Thanks again for supporting me on this indie publishing adventure!

How to Access Your Freebies

To access your free bonus materials:

1. Scan the QR code below using your phone's camera (or QR code scanner app).
2. Fill in the short form with your details.
3. Instantly download your bonus resources and sign up to our email list for more coloring pages, activity sheets, and other freebies weekly!

Possible Amazon Review?

As a small indie publisher, reviews are hard to come by, as many readers don't leave reviews even if these books have provided them with plenty of benefits.

I would love it if you could leave a review for the book on Amazon (and Goodreads, if you would like)! This will help me a ton and help me keep providing wonderful pieces of content for you all!

Sources of Information

As said in the introduction, I wanted to make this book different from other books on the market and actually show how this book is founded upon actual facts that you can search for yourself! Please take a look at the sources I used to help create this book. Keep in mind that information changes over time, and things may possibly not be the same!

American Academy of Pediatrics. https://www.aap.org/

American Heart Association. https://www.heart.org/

American Library Association. https://www.ala.org/

American Psychological Association. https://www.apa.org/

American Society for Bone and Mineral Research. https://www.asbmr.org/Default.aspx

American Society of Hematology. https://www.hematology.org/

American Veterinary Medicine Association. https://www.avma.org/

AnnualReports.com. https://www.annualreports.com/

AmeriCorps. https://americorps.gov/

Association for Psychological Science. https://www.psychologicalscience.org/

Bloomberg. https://www.bloomberg.com/

Bone Health and Osteoporosis Foundation. https://www.bonehealthandosteoporosis.org/

Carnegie Mellon University LearnLab. https://learnlab.org/

CDC (Centers for Disease Control and Prevention).
https://www.cdc.gov/

DARPA. https://www.darpa.mil/

Department of Agriculture, U.S. https://fdc.nal.usda.gov/

Department of Education, U.S. https://www.ed.gov/

Department of Energy, U.S. https://www.energy.gov/

Department of Homeland Security, U.S. https://www.fema.gov/

Department of Transportation, U.S.
https://www.transportation.gov/

Department of the Treasury, U.S. https://home.treasury.gov/

Duolingo. https://www.duolingo.com/

European Space Agency. https://www.esa.int/

European Southern Observatory. https://www.eso.org/public/

Ethnologue. https://www.ethnologue.com/

FIFA. https://www.fifa.com/en

Finnish National Agency for Education. https://www.oph.fi/en

Food and Agriculture Organization of the United Nations.
https://www.fao.org/home/en/

Frontiers. https://www.frontiersin.org/

FWS (Fish & Wildlife Service, U.S.). https://www.fws.gov/

Google. https://www.google.com

Government Offices of Sweden. https://www.government.se/

GPS.gov. https://www.gps.gov/

Guinness World Records. https://www.guinnessworldrecords.com/

Harvard Medical School. https://hms.harvard.edu/

Harvard T.H. Chan School of Public Health.
https://hsph.harvard.edu/

IBISWorld. https://www.ibisworld.com/

IEEE Microwave Theory and Technology Society. https://mtt.org/

International Air Transport Association. https://www.iata.org/

International Chess Federation. https://www.fide.com/

International Committee of the Red Cross. https://www.icrc.org/en

International Cricket Council. https://www.icc-cricket.com/

International Dairy Foods Association. https://www.idfa.org/

International Energy Agency. https://www.iea.org/

International Federation of Library Associations and Institutions.
https://www.ifla.org/

International Federation of Phonographic Industry.
https://www.ifpi.org/

International Maritime Association. https://www.imo.org/

International Monetary Fund. https://www.imf.org/en/Home

International Olympics Committee. https://www.olympics.com/ioc

International Renewable Energy Agency. https://www.irena.org/

International Skating Union. https://www.isu.org/

International Society for Horticultural Science.
https://www.ishs.org/

International Union for Conservation of Nature. https://iucn.org/

International Union for Convservation of Nature. https://iucn.org/

International Wildlife Fund. https://www.worldwildlife.org/

International World Trade Organization. https://www.wto.org/

International World Intellectual Property Organization. https://www.wipo.int/portal/en/index.html

IPCC (Intergovernmental Panel on Climate Change). https://www.ipcc.ch/

Koala Conservation Australia. https://koalaconservationaustralia.org.au/

MIT Museum. https://mitmuseum.mit.edu/

Ministry of Education, Culture, Sports, Science and Technology. https://www.mext.go.jp/en/

Microsoft. https://www.microsoft.com/en-us

NASA. https://www.nasa.gov/

NASA Technical Reports Server. https://ntrs.nasa.gov/

National Air and Space Museum. https://airandspace.si.edu/

National Center for Education Statistics. https://nces.ed.gov/

National Dance Council of America. https://www.ndca.org/

National Education Association. https://www.nea.org/

National Geographic. https://www.nationalgeographic.com/

National Highway Traffic Safety Administration. https://www.nhtsa.gov/

National Institute of Neurological Disorders and Stroke, NIH. https://www.ninds.nih.gov/

National Oceanic and Atmospheric Administration. https://www.noaa.gov/

National Park Service, U.S. https://www.nps.gov/index.htm

National Wildlife Federation. https://www.nwf.org/

NIH National Library of Medicine. https://www.ncbi.nlm.nih.gov/

NHTSA (National Highway Traffic Safety Administration). https://www.nhtsa.gov/

NASA Technical Reports Server. https://ntrs.nasa.gov/

OECD (Organisation for Economic Co-operation and Development). https://www.oecd.org/

Oxford Academic. https://academic.oup.com/

Pew Research Center. https://www.pewresearch.org/

Psychology Today. https://www.psychologytoday.com/us

Salk Institute for Biological Studies. https://www.salk.edu/

ScienceDirect. https://www.sciencedirect.com/

Smithsonian. https://www.si.edu/

Solid Waste Association of North America. https://swana.org/

Space.com. https://www.space.com/

Springer Nature. https://link.springer.com/

Stockholm International Peace Research Institute. https://www.sipri.org/

Statista. https://www.statista.com/

The Journal of Nutrition. https://jn.nutrition.org/

U.K. National Literacy Trust. https://literacytrust.org.uk/

U.K. Government Website. https://www.gov.uk/

U.N. Environmental Programme. https://www.unep.org/

U.N. Official Website. https://www.un.org/en/

U.N. Sustainable Development Solutions Network.
https://www.unsdsn.org/

UNESCO. https://uis.unesco.org/

UNICEF. https://www.unicef.org/

U.S. Bureau of Engraving & Printing. https://www.bep.gov/

U.S. Bureau of Labor Statistics. https://www.bls.gov/

U.S. Census Bureau. https://www.census.gov/

U.S. Centers for Disease Control and Prevention.
https://www.cdc.gov/

U.S. Department of Education. https://www.ed.gov/

U.S. Department of Energy. https://www.energy.gov/

U.S. Department of Homeland Security. https://www.fema.gov/

U.S. Department of the Treasury. https://home.treasury.gov/

U.S. Department of Transportation.
https://www.transportation.gov/

U.S. Environmental Protection Agency. https://www.epa.gov/

U.S. Federal Aviation Administration. https://www.faa.gov/

U.S. Fish & Wildlife Service. https://www.fws. gov/

U.S. National Park Service. https://www.nps.gov/index.htm

U.S. Patent and Trademark Office. https://www.uspto.gov/

U.S. Treasury Department. https://home.treasury.gov/

Wiley Online Library. https://onlinelibrary.wiley.com/

World Bank Group. https://www.worldbank.org/ext/en/home

World Economic Forum. https://www.weforum.org/

World Federation of the Deaf. https://wfdeaf.org/

World Health Organization. https://www.who.int/

World Intellectual Property Organization.
https://www.wipo.int/portal/en/index.html

World Meteorological Organization. https://wmo.int/

World Trade Organization. https://www.wto.org/

World Wildlife Fund. https://www.worldwildlife.org/

Acknowledgements

Freepik. https://www.freepik.com/

Getcovers. https://getcovers.com/

Made in the USA
Middletown, DE
31 March 2025

73518713R00085